THE KALAHARI KILLINGS

THE TRUE STORY OF A WARTIME DOUBLE MURDER IN BOTSWANA, 1943

JONATHAN LAVERICK

The History Press

Front cover image: © IWM

First published 2015

The History Press
The Mill, Brimscombe Port
Stroud, Gloucestershire, GL5 2QG
www.thehistorypress.co.uk

© Jonathan Laverick, 2015

The right of Jonathan Laverick to be identified as the Author
of this work has been asserted in accordance with the
Copyright, Designs and Patents Act 1988.

British Library Cataloguing in Publication Data.
A catalogue record for this book is available from the British Library.

ISBN 978 0 7509 5665 9

Typesetting and origination by The History Press
Printed in Great Britain

CONTENTS

Introduction	4	Friday 29 September	161
		Summary of the Case	
Part 1 – Training	9	for the Prosecution	172
England, 1940	10	Summary of the Case	
Bechuanaland, 1940	17	for the Defence: Kelly	178
Scotland, 1941	25	Summary of the Case	
Bechuanaland, 1941	29	for the Defence: Fraenkel	180
Russia, 1941	38	Judgement	184
Bechuanaland, 1941	45		
Egypt, 1942	53	**Part 5 – Aftermath**	**189**
Bechuanaland, 1943	62	The Royal Air Force	190
Rhodesia, 1943	71	'A Striking Example of	
		British Justice'	193
		Talifang	201
Part 2 – Missing	**77**	The Edwards Family	202
RAF Induna	78	'The Ten Thousand Men'	204
RAF Kumalo	85		
Final Flight	93	**Part 6 – Postscript**	**207**
		Tshekedi Khama's Downfall	
Part 3 – Search	**99**	and Seretse's Rise	208
Overdue	100	Impact on the Bushmen	212
Missing	102	Twai Twai	215
		The Ten Thousand:	
Part 4 – Trial	**105**	Rre Molatlhwe	216
Lobatsi	106	RATG	219
Monday 25 September	109	Gordon's Fiancée	222
Tuesday 26 September	128	The Hurricane of the Lake	223
Wednesday 27 September	138		
Thursday 28 September	146	Index	225

INTRODUCTION

I first came across this story when researching the history of a Tiger Moth owned by one of the parents of a student of mine, here in Botswana. The little de Havilland trainer was important because a brief internet search led to the story of the murder of an RAF pilot by giraffe-eating Bushmen after crashing his Tiger Moth. It was a bizarre tale that had all the elements of a good book, even if, as I was to find out, most of it was wrong.

Hooked, I started to dig deeper and quickly found that multiple versions of the same tale existed, but the details changed with each new version I unearthed. Indeed, Tony Park's novel *African Sky* opens with a pair of Bushmen murdering a Harvard pilot in Bechuanaland. Fortunately, my search coincided with that of Chris Watkins in England, who was building his family tree. He had had a great uncle 'that had flown Spitfires in the war', but when he applied for Gordon Edwards' records he found that he had been killed while training in Rhodesia. More research on his part discovered that Gordon had in fact been the centre of one of the strangest murder cases in African history. Not only that, but the story had been the subject of an academic paper by an American professor.

Robert Hitchcock is one of the world's leading authorities on indigenous peoples, especially the San of southern Africa. In 1975, however, he was a young researcher who had too much time on his hands during his stays in Gaborone, the capital of Botswana. He spent this free time in the Botswana National Archives looking into issues that involved Bushmen. One file that caught his imagination was that of *Rex v. Twai Twai Molele et al.* as it included a lot of information, including diagrams, on how the Tyua group of Bushmen had lived and hunted in the early parts of the twentieth century. This formed the basis for his paper entitled 'Kuacaca: An Early Case of Ethnoarcheology in the Northern Kalahari'. The file also told the story of the fate of Gordon Edwards and his co-pilot, Walter Adamson.

Having made contact with Chris and Bob, the next step was to visit the national archives in Botswana to see whether the court documents were available. The good news was the case notes existed still, but the bad news was that they were in the process of being moved when I first applied to see them. While waiting for them to be found, I started going through files only loosely connected to the case and I found a lot more information about how nearly 10,000 men from Botswana had volunteered to fight in the Second World War. The aftermath of the trial was also discussed in detail, as it came close to causing a major diplomatic incident, if not a minor war of its own.

When the court documents surfaced, all 240 pages of them, I was amazed by what I found. Having lived in Botswana for sixteen years and enjoyed its friendly, easy-going atmosphere, it was hard to match the casual brutality of the alleged murders with my experience of the country. It was also hard to believe that the High Court in sleepy Lobatse was once the focus for the world's press, with the story of the murders appearing in newspapers all over the Empire. That coverage was itself a testament to the curiousness of the case. The fact that the trial got such extensive attention while Allied troops were still fighting their way through Europe was another indicator of the sensational nature of the killings.

Contact with various ORAFS (Old Rhodesian Air Force Sods) added detail to the Rhodesian Air Training Group's role in teaching nearly 10,000 pilots from across the Empire during the Second World War, while a visit to the RAF Museum's reading room gave access to the training syllabi and a range of log-books that belonged to Gordon Edwards' contemporaries. The National Archives at Kew added the London side of the story as well as more newspaper coverage from the era. Tracking down suitable photographs also took up some considerable, but thoroughly enjoyable, time.

Finally, a visit to Bulawayo and the airfield Gordon had last taken off from, and a trip to the salt pans in northern Botswana where he lost his life, completed my research. My only disappointment was being unable to trace any surviving members of Walter Adamson's family, the other pilot who was killed. Perhaps the publication of this book will lead to further information becoming available.

I would like to thank the following, in no particular order, for their help and assistance during the production of this book. Joanna Poweska, my wife, for her undying support and encouragement. Robert Hitchcock for his endless knowledge and his willingness to share his research to an amazing extent. Chris Watkins and the Edwards family for their enthusiasm for the project, along with the time and information they donated. Tony Park, for sharing his sources so quickly, The National Archives of Botswana and The National Archives of the United Kingdom, two institutions that could not be any more different in terms of size and technology, but which are both full of the most interesting documents and are staffed by the most helpful people in the world, something appreciated by nervous first-time visitors. To those who were willing to share photographs, often from departed loved ones, usually only asking for credit for fathers or grandfathers, I am especially grateful. The late Eddy Norris certainly deserves a mention. Finally, to all those that take the time to maintain websites that commemorate those that made such big sacrifices during the Second World War, a big thank you, both for sharing information so easily, but also for keeping alive the memories of those who barely made it out of their teens over seventy years on.

Incidentally, the Tiger Moth that started this story was an ex-Indian Air Force machine. If I had found that out sooner, this would have been a very short book.

A Note on Language

Setswana is not the easiest of languages to learn and I would not wish the reader to lose too much enjoyment from its overuse. However, the following explanations may be of some use.

The plural is usually given by *Ba* and singular by *Mo*. So the people of Botswana are Batswana, the people of the Ngwato tribe are *Bangwato*. A single Batswana is a *Motswana*. *Dummela* is the usual greeting, almost always followed by *Rra* or *Mma* (sir/madam).

In the text I refer to Tswana kings and chiefs and these can be considered interchangeable. The Setswana word *Kgosi* certainly implies royal blood, but the British administration tended to use 'chief' for reasons that were then obvious.

The Bushmen go by a variety of names and the reasons for this are explained later. The word 'Bushman' did at one point go out of favour, but many Bushmen find the alternatives no friendlier. The Setswana term *Sarwa* is used in some parts, with *Mosarwa* being singular and *Basarwa* plural. Other common alternatives are *San* or *Khoi-San*. The major problem with all of these terms is that they are often used as a catch-all phrase to describe often quite different groups of people.

Place names are given as those at the time of the incidents described, so Botswana is usually described as the Bechuanaland Protectorate.

TRAINING

ENGLAND, 1940

On 23 May 1940, a Miles Magister skimmed its way toward Calais at very low level on a desperate rescue mission, its escort of two Spitfires slightly above and behind, the cold waves of the English Channel barely a couple of feet below.

The two-seat trainer was on its way to pick up the commanding officer of 74 Squadron who had found himself marooned in France in the middle of a huge and chaotic retreat. His own Spitfire had been forced down hours earlier by a Messerschmitt Bf 109, as his squadron tried to protect the British troops heading for the small port town of Dunkirk. Experienced pilots were so valuable to the Royal Air Force at this point that the order for his recovery had come from the very top of 11 Group.

Leatheart, the pilot of the Magister, made a textbook landing, and picked up his passenger before opening his throttle wide. The trainer picked up speed, bounced and was airborne. Instantly there was

A Miles Magister, as flown by Leatheart on his daring mission to rescue his CO. (*Doug Claydon/New Dawn images*)

the rat-a-tat-tat of machine-gun bullets hitting the small plane. Leatheart cut the engine and slammed his craft back down to earth as a 109 flashed past. As the German climbed past, smoke billowed from its engine before it rolled over and dived into the sea with an almighty splash. Another 109 hit the ground inside the airfield perimeter as Leatheart and his shaken senior passenger threw themselves hurriedly into a rather muddy ditch. A Messerschmitt roared down out of the clouds with a Spitfire on its tail before the gloom swallowed both of them again. In the distance an explosion marked the end of the last 109. After waiting for five minutes, the Magister set off again to deliver its valuable cargo to RAF Hornchurch.

Al Deere was the pilot of one of the escorting Spitfires that claimed two of the 109s and he was a perfect example of the reach of the British Empire. A New Zealander who had joined the RAF three years before, he had only been flying Spitfires for five months, but he was already becoming something of a star.

Deere was fortunate to have made it even this far in his flying career, lucky not to have been killed in an air crash two years earlier. A keen amateur boxer, he had been selected to join the RAF team that was going to tour South Africa. Fortunately for him, his flight training took precedence and he remained in England. Fortunate because, after competing in Bulawayo, one of the three South African Air Force Airspeed Envoys carrying the team back to Pretoria disappeared amid heavy cloud over the Limpopo River that marked the border with Bechuanaland. After an intensive search, the wreckage and bodies of the six crew and passengers were found just inside the protectorate at Balemo. The accident claimed a final victim when one of the Bechuanaland Protectorate policemen, who was part of the search party, cut himself badly during the search. The officer, Dennis Reilly, developed gangrene and died not long afterward.

Within a week of the daring Dunkirk rescue flight, Deere himself was shot down over Belgium by a German bomber he was attacking and had to make his way home on foot via the evacuations at Dunkirk. This cannot have been an easy journey because at the time the RAF was not popular with the army, who felt the air force was not doing enough to protect the troops on the beaches and feelings were running high, to say the least.

Al Deere was awarded the Distinguished Flying Cross (DFC), along with the other two rescue pilots, on 12 June 1940 with his citation making mention of the fact that he had already, even before the Battle of Britain started, shot down five enemy aircraft. Despite writing off nine aircraft, either crashed or shot down, Al Deere finished his career in the RAF as an Air Commodore in 1967, having added a Distinguished Service Order (DSO) and a bar to his DFC.

Perhaps it was the heroics of Deere, and others like him, that encouraged a 19-year-old Welshman by the name of Gordon Edwards to join the RAF. The lure of excitement and adventure must have been tempting to the blue-eyed, brown-haired, lanky teenager who was about to start a career as a clerk in the small town of Porth in Glamorganshire.

Gordon Edwards was born on 25 April 1921 in the small village of Ynyshir and he was the pride and joy of his mother, Sarah. Ynyshir, on the Taff Valley Railway, consisted of little more than a square of miners' cottages. Nestled in the Rhondda Valley, it was a typical of the colliery settlements that had sprung up on previously sparsely populated agricultural land. Despite its small size, the village boasted several churches of various dominations, but Gordon's English mother took him to Porth to have him baptised into the Church of England.

Originally from Birmingham, Sarah Edwards had moved to South Wales with her Scottish husband. However, the union was not a happy one and Gordon was brought up by his mother in the small village of Pontyclun, farther down the valley towards Cardiff. This small hamlet had consisted of only four or five households before the coming of the South Wales Railway in

1851, which opened up commercial opportunities for mining, and by the end of that decade there was a flourishing colliery and iron mine in operation. This drew workers from far afield, particularly from Cornwall where the tin-mining industry was in terminal decline. By the turn of the century it had developed into a small, but bustling, working-class industrial town boasting both rugby and football clubs. As well as mining, there were various light industries, including a brewery producing several hundred barrels of beer a week to quench the thirst of the miners.

Despite separating from her volatile husband, Sarah never divorced, and brought up Gordon and his elder sister, Muriel, alone. At the same time she looked after her widowed father who lived with the young family, creating what must have been a tightly knit unit. Certainly Sarah developed a reputation of being a strong-willed and tough woman, typical perhaps of many such women in mining villages up and down the country. Despite the presence of her father, nobody was left in any doubt that she was the head of the household.

Sarah's brother had followed her to Wales from Birmingham and was working as a chauffeur at the nearby Miskin Manor. Although claims of a manor at the site went back nearly a thousand years, the current building dated to 1864 when David Williams built the large Tudor-style mansion. According to local legend, the Williams family had made significant money from South African gold, as well as having interests in the regional iron ore mines.

Gordon was a tall but thin young boy who was protected by his mother, who considered him too frail for a future in the mines. Indeed, Sarah Edwards considered the local schools too tough for her favourite child and a combination of her will power and Gordon's academic ability saw him win a place at Cowbridge Grammar School, where he appears to have done well. His mother's pride was immense, especially as she was well aware of the fact that her own education had ended at the age of 10. Despite his mother's fears, Gordon obviously got caught up in some youthful scrapes as his later service records mention a scar below his right eye, two scars on the back of the scalp, as well as further scarring to both knees.

During his time at school, Sarah decided to move the family to Miskin. This move suited Gordon as he could join the Miskin Manor Cricket Club. During school holidays he played in the youth team alongside Glyn Williams, the heir to the Williams fortune. This fortune was obviously quite significant as the manor had been rebuilt after a serious fire in 1922 without too much interruption. By the end of his schooling, Gordon got the occasional game for the senior team. This was quite an achievement as the small village team had developed an impressive reputation, despite its limited facilities. Gordon would have changed, and for that matter taken lunch and tea, in tented facilities while taking on special guest teams, including Glamorgan County. The scorers had slightly better accommodation, being homed in an old toll house that had once stood at the entrance to Pontyclun. The cost of the relocation had been met in full by Sir Rhys Williams. It is clear that Gordon had a passion for the game, while his mother no doubt appreciated the fact that cricket matched her goals for her son, much more than football or rugby would have done. The make-up of the pre-war Miskin team is socially interesting, comprised as it was of miners' sons, a police sergeant and the heir to a mining fortune who had just finished his schooling at Eton. Dai Hammond made several centuries for Miskin before being called up for Nottinghamshire.

By the time Gordon left school, his sister was already married with a daughter of her own. Gordon became very close to her in-laws and extremely fond of his niece, Rosalind. Tall and handsome, his dark hair setting off his blue eyes, the young Welshman was blossoming. Yet by the time of his eighteenth birthday, it was clear that the storm clouds were gathering and that the world would soon be plunged into a conflict that would dwarf the Great War of his parents' generation.

Three weeks after Dunkirk, Gordon found himself at the RAF recruitment centre at Uxbridge, having travelled to London without telling his mother. In fact, he had had a service medical a week earlier and had been declared Category II, which ruled out any idea of being a pilot. The next eight weeks saw him shuttled between various processing centres while the Air Force decided what to do with the young Welshman. This gave Gordon several opportunities to visit home and give Sarah time to get used to the idea. It can be assumed, that after her initial shock, his mother did not share Gordon's disappointment at being kept on the ground. With the Battle of Britain underway and pilots being lost or, worse in many eyes, burnt unrecognisably, ground crew must have looked a safer option to Mrs Edwards.

Eventually, towards the end of September, Gordon was sent to No. 6 School of Technical Training at RAF Hednesford. This camp was situated seven miles outside of Stafford and was a relatively new facility, having only being completed the previous year. It was a huge site, with its own hospital, post office, cinema, two firing ranges and three churches, but it had no runway and consequently no airworthy aircraft. It was intended to be a short sharp shock of an introduction into service life, with discipline forming a large part of this. Marching, drills, physical exercise and general 'square bashing' were combined with education. In Gordon's case this was mechanical, learning the basics of how to service, maintain and fix the latest technological masterpieces that formed the Royal Air Force's front line. Many of his instructors were graduates of RAF Halton, home of the original apprentice airmen scheme. This training centre had been set up by Hugh Trenchard in the 1920s to ensure a supply of highly trained ground crew and enjoyed a remarkable reputation, its alumni being universally known as 'Trenchard's brats'.

Although Hednesford was new and had good amenities, accommodation was still basic. Gordon would have shared a large wooden hut with nineteen other raw recruits, something of a shock for a young man who had been considered too frail for his local school. This certainly was something of a coming of age. He would have met men from all over the UK and Gordon would have learned to make friends quickly. The village of Hednesford was within walking distance and the local pubs would have played their part in this male bonding.

After four months intensive training, Gordon Edwards left the Technical School as a qualified mechanic. In addition, he would have had a better understanding of RAF traditions.

BECHUANALAND, 1940

A small dot moved slowly across the huge metallic blue dome that formed the roof to the Kalahari Desert. The modern aeroplane, thousands of feet above the sand, merely served to emphasise the unchanging land known locally as the Kgalagadi or 'The Great Thirstland'. A country similar in size to France, Bechuanaland was home to less than 250,000 people in 1940 and the landscape gave clues as to why this was so. The vast Kalahari covered nearly four-fifths of the protectorate, with rain being limited to the devilishly hot summer months that ran from October to April. Only in the top western corner did the magnificent inland delta of the Okavango give any relief from the stunted bush that dotted the rest of the country.

Bechuanaland had always been something of an outlier in the British Empire, and visitors often left its barren land with the feeling that it had remained a separate country largely because nobody wanted it. This was especially true of anybody who came during the harsh dry season, when visiting British officials would look on in wonder at how any of the thousands of cattle could survive such conditions. This impression of 'unwantedness' was wide of the mark, however, and the story of how it became that rarest thing, a British Protectorate, is a fascinating one.

The Tsodilo Hills that mark the far north-western corner of the country had been inhabited for at least 19,000 years, with evidence left in caves by generations of the original inhabitants. These were the San, the Baswara, the Khoi or simply the Bushmen, and for the next 17,000 years they were the sole guardians of the land, but the next two millennia would see them forced into the harshest parts of the country or become little more than serfs and all but written out of history.

Often thought of as hunter-gatherers, these first inhabitants had, by the second century AD, started to keep livestock, definitely sheep and probably cattle, and some groups started to live in settled villages. While hunting and gathering of wild food formed an important part of life, it was now a supplement to their livestock and crop growing. Knowledge of pot-making seems to have arrived at the same time as the domestic animals, and it is probable that these had arrived through trade with people from East Africa.

Perhaps following on from this trade, Bantu-speaking people started to trickle down both sides of the Kalahari around AD 300, bringing with them knowledge of iron working. Originally from the Cameroon region of West Africa, these black Africans had spread to the Great Lakes area and it was probably here that they acquired the knowledge of millet and sorghum, and possibly gained cattle too. Others had travelled down the west coast and probably relied more on goats. Few in number, they appear to have had peaceful relations with the already present Khoisan, trading and inter-marrying. There also seems to have been borrowing from each other's beliefs and customs as the Bantu continued to spread south, into what is now South Africa.

The start of the second millennium saw a rise of competing Bantu chiefdoms. These involved various cattle-herding peoples who would supplement their food with meat gained from hunting. One major group settled around the Serowe area, with a capital at Toutswe Hill that supported kraals of cattle and goats in surrounding villages. The Toutswe would hunt into the Kalahari to the west and trade with the growing civilisations to the east. Shells from the distant Indian Ocean were used as currency in these early transactions, and these found their way all around the Kalahari region.

The Toutswe were eventually conquered by their trading partners, the Mapungubwe, sometime in the thirteenth century, but while Toutswe was abandoned, other villages survived. The Mapungubwe themselves would be soon incorporated into Great Zimbabwe, a civilization made rich by their control of the Shashe gold trade.

Great Zimbabwe and its successor, the Batua state, controlled not only the gold trade but also salt from the great Makgadikgadi Pans. When this empire collapsed, the Batua people in Botswana became known as the Kalanga and inhabited the north-east of the country.

The scene was then set for the rise of the Tswana. By the seventeenth century the Sotho or Tswana people stretched from the Transvaal in modern South Africa to the current Namibian border. These descendants from the early eastern stream of Bantu settlers were now formed into related cattle keeping clans. As land was overgrazed they would move on to better pastures, eventually bringing them to south-eastern Botswana. These clans, tribes or *merafe* shared customs and a belief system based on a creator god, Modimo. Other lesser gods were spirits of their earliest ancestors. They also had a class-based system, led by the *Kgosi*, or chief, and the royal family. People from other Batswana tribes who had joined the *merafe* were next, followed by people from non-Batswana clans. The Khoisan were known for the first time as *Basarwa* and these were never admitted to the *merafe*. Instead, they were often treated as slaves, forced to work in the fields or to herd cattle for little reward. These groups varied in size, but the largest probably had around 10,000 members by around 1800. Despite this, the Batswana had little political or military might.

Difaqane is the name given to the disaster that befell the Batswana next. Literally meaning 'hordes of people' it might not be a perfect description, but it does give an impression of the chaos it brought. The causes of this dislocation were many, but all of them put inward pressure on the Batswana tribes. The slave trade was flourishing, and Maputo and Delagoa Bay on the east coast had become major centres in the trade of humans. There was money to be made and African chiefs were encouraged to raid each other for slaves, being armed by Europeans to do so. These raids also meant that crops and cattle were stolen. Griqua bandits raided the area just to the south of Botswana, often selling their slaves to white farmers.

Far to the south, Shaka Zulu's reign caused panic in the tribes above his expanding empire. Many of these fled north and north-westwards, some travelling as far as Tanzania before settling. On their journey they raided Batswana settlements for food and cattle. Worse was to follow, as Mzilikazi broke away from Shaka's rule with 300 warriors. On his way to the Magaliesburg Mountains, to the west of where Pretoria would be built, he collected a veritable horde of people. He cleared his new land of any potential enemies, including many Batswana. From here, Mzilikazi sent out raiding parties for both cattle and people. The Batswana clans could not cope with these constant raids and many broke into smaller groups and moved further into what would become Botswana. The whole region was full of small wandering bands of people, looking for food and safety.

The expansion of Dutch-speaking white farmers, the Boers, up from the Cape, avoiding British rule, was an additional pressure on the peoples of southern Africa. Believing in their God-given right to the land, some pushed as far as the Transvaal, settling on what appeared to be empty land. In fact, the region they chose had until recently been the home to Batswana before Mzilikazi had chased them away. Mzilikazi soon learned of the arrival of the Boers and sent two of his regiments to deal with them. Despite losing their cattle, by circling their wagons the farmers managed to survive this first attack. Relieved by a new party of Boers, the farmers went on the attack, aided by a significant party of Batswana warriors. The Batswana were officially there to help the white men recover their cattle but there must have been an element of revenge for them. Mzilikazi was being harried by Zulus to the south and a steadily increasing number of Boers to the east. He decided to make a move north, terrorising eastern Botswana as he passed through.

This disruption lasted for nearly fifty years, but by 1840 the Tswana kingdoms of the Ngwaketse, Kwena and Ngwato were in place to form the beginnings of a new state. These had been formed by chiefs gathering up their people, who had been spread far and wide by the troubles, and by incorporating smaller *merafe*. After the *Difaqane* the Kgosi realised that the only way to protect themselves from outside influences was to be well armed. The trade of ivory paid for guns, which allowed for more successful hunting. Soon the great elephant herds around the Orange and Molopo Rivers had been destroyed. This hunting moved gradually northwards, until there was no big game left in the southern half of Botswana. This growing trade route, which also saw fur and ostrich feathers make their way down wagon routes to the Cape Colony more than 1,000 miles away, also attracted missionaries. These included the famous Doctor David Livingstone. He was responsible for the conversion of King Sechele I, chief of the Kwena in Molepolele, although Christianity struggled to catch on with his tribesmen. Livingstone was also responsible for the first church and school to be built in Botswana, at Koboleng, not far from the current capital, Gaborone. These were destroyed by Boer farmers after they had fallen out with their recent Tswana allies.

A little further north, a German missionary by the name of Heinrich Schulenburg worked to convert members of the Ngwato at their capital, Shoshong. In his second year he carried out his first nine baptisms, which included Khama and Khamane, two sons of the king, Sekgoma. When the London Missionary Society (LMS) replaced the German in 1862, the two boys were enrolled in the school run by Elizabeth Price. Khama's popularity and easy disposition were noted and he would become a star LMS pupil in more ways than one. However, political interference by the LMS almost cost him his birthright. The missionaries were frustrated that the king, Sekgoma, refused to convert and did not want to upset his ancestors by ending tribal traditions, such as initiations for young men and bride price for women. This, along with Khama's marriage to a Christian, drove a rift between the king and his heir. With LMS help, Sekgoma was dethroned and a Christian outsider

imposed; however, all this succeeded in achieving was the reconcili-
ation between father and son, and together they soon had Sekgoma
back on the throne. The peace did not last long and Khama took his
followers to Serowe and from there launched an attack on his father.
Within a month Khama was King Khama III.

With Shoshong becoming less fertile and suffering from unre-
liable water supplies, the Bangwato relocated to Khama's new
stronghold of Serowe. From here Khama became widely known
as an enlightened leader, introducing new Western technology
such as wagons and ox-drawn ploughs. He also stuck with his
Christian faith, cracking down on initiation services and traditional beliefs as well as prohibiting alcohol from his territories.
The LMS became the state church, with Khama banning other
missionaries and the construction of competing churches.

Just as stability was restored, Khama was faced with two new
problems in the form of competing Europeans. Germans were
encroaching from German South-West Africa (modern Namibia),
while Boers were making constant raids from the south-east, partly
with an eye to possible gold fields. Khama appealed to the British

Khama and his headmen around 1882. (*Council for World Mission archive,
SOAS Library – CWM/LMS/Africa Photographs Box 6 file 42 25*)

who considered the Tswana as allies against the Boers, and a protectorate was declared in 1880. This initially encompassed the lands as far north as Khama's kingdom before being extended to the Chobe River five years later, finalising the borders of Bechuanland. Somewhat amazingly, the newest country in the Empire was soon the scene of Britain's first use of military air power when a balloon regiment was sent to help counter Boer raids in 1883.

The new country was still under threat though, this time from a megalomaniac Englishman. Cecil Rhodes was already using the road through Bechuanaland to reach Zimbabwe, soon to be Rhodesia, and had his eye on the empty spaces of the Kalahari. The LMS helped organise a direct appeal to the British people by shipping the three most important chiefs, Sechele I, Khama III and Bathoen I, to the UK. Here, assisted by W.C. Willoughby of the LMS, the three kings toured the country and caused quite a stir, as can be imagined. With public opinion on their side they returned home with a rare victory for Africans. Rhodes and the British South African Company had to settle for only land rights to build a railway through the eastern side of the country to Bulawayo.

Despite many Batswana fighting with the British in the Anglo-Boer war, the British Government maintained an arm's length approach to the protectorate. With the formation of South Africa in 1910, the British promised that the three High Commission Territories, Bechuanaland, Lesotho and Swaziland, would one day be handed over to the Union. This terrified the Batswana chiefs, who had first-hand experience of how the Boers treated Africans. With the rise of Hertzog, and an increasingly racist Boer regime in the south, the British secretary of state for the colonies made a visit to the three territories in the mid-1920s. He left in no doubt of the view of the Batswana chiefs. Bechuanaland maintained popular support in the UK Parliament, despite the cost of an admittedly tiny administration, and a promise of consultation before any decision was made. Relationships between the administration and the chiefs were generally good, although the fact that the administrative capital was Mafeking, over the border in South Africa, gives some idea of how important the British considered the territory.

Khama III ruled until his death at 87 in 1923 when he was succeeded by his son Sekgoma II. Unfortunately, the new king survived in the post only a little over a year, leaving an infant called Seretse as heir. Given the new king's age it was decided that Seretse's uncle Tshekedi should act as regent – a decision that would have far reaching consequences.

SCOTLAND, 1941

A Hurricane flopped onto the grass runway and taxied in towards a waiting group of pilots, but they ignored its engine's dying coughs as they gazed upwards in unison at the graceful shape approaching. They had waited a long time for this moment, and had been joined in their vigil by most of the ground crew. With a flick of its elliptical wing the newcomer rolled over and dived towards the airfield, sending the onlookers scattering in all directions. Loops and rolls followed before a perfect three-point landing saw the first of a new breed join 111 Squadron. The Supermarine Spitfire had arrived and Gordon Edwards was as excited as anybody else on the Scottish airfield.

Treble-one Squadron had endured a busy start to the war and were having a well deserved rest on the east coast of Scotland. Formed in Palestine during the First World War, the unit had gained fame as the first to re-equip with Hawker Hurricanes when the first examples arrived at Northolt in December 1937. The Hurricane was a huge leap forward for the Royal Air Force, replacing decidedly obsolete biplanes, and 111 were understandably proud of their new mounts. Their commanding officer had added to their air of superiority when he flew a Hurricane from Turnhouse, Edinburgh to Northolt, London at an average speed of 409 miles per hour. Given the fact the maximum speed of the early Hurricanes was only 320 mph, this was clearly weather assisted and the feat earned the Squadron Leader the nickname of 'Downwind Gillan' in the British press.

When the war started, 111 were lucky to be one of the few Hurricane squadrons not to be sent to France to cover the ill-fated British Expeditionary Force. Instead, their main targets in the opening months of the conflict were rogue barrage balloons. The squadron shot down at least eleven of these inflated monsters that had escaped their bounds during the first six weeks of the war. A move to Northumberland was followed by a move further north to Drem to give cover to the Navy base at Scapa Flow. However, the squadron had returned south in time for the Battle of France. Though based once more at Northolt, the squadron often operated from forward bases in France to try and slow down the German advance. This gave the squadron its first taste of combat against fighter opposition. During the brief fight for France the squadron was credited with thirteen kills, but in return it had sacrificed five of its Hurricanes and, more importantly, three of its pilots. Like Al Deere's 74 Squadron, 111 was then involved in the evacuation of Dunkirk, doing their best to provide aerial cover for the soldiers making their way to the beaches. The fact that much of the combat took place out of sight of the troops led to accusations by some in the Army that the Air Force was not doing its job.

With France conquered and most of Europe under Nazi control, the Germans looked across the English Channel to their next target. The *Wehrmacht* knew that this thin strip of water provided a formidable obstacle, one that without control of the air would be impossible to overcome. The scene was set for the Battle of Britain.

During the battle, whenever possible, 111 Squadron and its Hurricanes were targeted against German bombers, leaving the Messerschmitts to the sleeker Spitfires. The unit earned a reputation for daring head-on attacks against the massed Heinkels, Dorniers and Junkers. By the middle of August, the Luftwaffe was targeting RAF airfields, but Northolt escaped the worst of the bombing. Perhaps this was due to the base commander, Group Captain Stanley Vincent, who had decided to camouflage the station to blend in with its London suburbs. Hangers had been painted to look like houses, complete with gardens, and a stream painted across the main runway. During this period 111 also operated from a number of satellite airfields around London, such as Croydon and Debden. If they were relatively lucky on the ground, then life in the air was taking its toll. The squadron suffered heavy losses during August and when the Luftwaffe switched targets to concentrate on London, the squadron became busier still.

As the Battle of Britain reached its climax, the battered and bruised unit was pulled from the front line. During the battle, 111 claimed forty-seven enemy aircraft destroyed, but it was the loss of eighteen Hurricanes in a matter of weeks that was crucial in the decision to rest the squadron by transferring it to Scotland.

Gordon Edwards had joined the squadron shortly after the move north and he must have been in awe of some of the pilots he would have met. These were battle-hardened veterans, men he had read about in the newspapers. The same went for the ground crews that he worked with. They were experienced and knew what it was to work under fire and to lose pilots and aircraft that it was their job to look after. In short, this was an ideal posting for a newly trained recruit with a lot still to learn.

Life at Dyce was quiet, giving plenty of time for Gordon to settle into squadron life. The same went for the large number of replacement pilots. Regular patrols were flown, but action was rarely seen. During the Battle of Britain the station had been raided by German bombers based in Norway with little effect and the Nazis seemed little inclined to repeat the process. Despite the lack of threat, a decoy airfield was maintained at nearby Harestone Moss. This consisted of a generator-powered flare path and moving lights, to give the impression of a 'live' base at night.

Aberdeen, Scotland's third largest city, was nearby with its impressive nineteenth-century infrastructure. With its shipbuilding and fishing industries, it offered the entertainments to be found in any port city. Aberdeen also has some stunning beaches, although how much time Gordon spent walking along them during a Scottish winter is not known.

His time in Scotland would have been both pleasant and useful. The lack of serious enemy action gave Gordon time to learn the workings of a modern fighter aircraft inside out. The replacement of the slightly dated Hurricane, with its thick wings and fabric-covered fuselage, by the state-of-the-art Spitfire would have provided a new challenge at an ideal time in his career. Although a long way from the south Wales valleys, communication with home by letter was a regular occurrence. Gordon not only wrote to his mother and sister, but also to his sister's parents-in-law. During extended periods of leave it was possible to visit his family, although the journey across the country in packed, blacked-out and often disrupted trains must have been a tortuous one. However difficult these trips must have been, they were also fruitful ones as around this time Gordon seems to have developed a special friendship with a young lady back home.

After six months with a crack fighter squadron, Gordon must have worn his uniform with pride, feeling himself to be something of a well-trained veteran.

BECHUANALAND, 1941

In villages all over Bechuanaland, selected young men underwent drill instruction, often within view of the 'war fields' that had sprung up around the country. The sun beat down on sweaty bodies marching up and down, round and round, presenting arms and standing to attention, all under the watchful eye of the uniformed native instructor. Soon there would be 10,000 Batswana under arms.

The response to this conflict was in contrast to the First World War. Bechuanaland had been largely untouched by the devastation of the 'War to end all Wars'. The chiefs had supported the British, perhaps hoping that in return they would get some protection from white settlers and remain outside of the Union of South Africa. Some, such as Linchwe I, Seepapitso and Sechele II, wanted to show their loyalty to Britain by providing troops. Khama III was one of the few who were not keen on sending men to fight, fearing his men would only be given menial tasks. Despite this, he did send money to aid the cause. Only around 500 men joined the army as they were generally required to serve in the Native Labour Contingent of the disliked South African Army, where they suffered racial discrimination. In France, some Batswana were confined to compounds intended for prisoners of war when not on duty. Despite receiving thanks from King George V upon his visit to Abbeville in 1917, during which he called them 'part of my great Armies which are fighting for the liberty and freedom of my subjects of all races and creed throughout the Empire', after the war many Batswana refused to accept their medals.

The war memorial in modern-day Gaborone lists only one casualty from this conflict, a police messenger known by the single name of Jonas. The only Bechuanaland war grave is in the Milton

Cemetery in Portsmouth, where a headstone marks the sacrifice of Private Willie Pampiri Tlhomelang who drowned when his troopship, the SS *Mendi*, sank after a collision in the English Channel. Tlhomelang was one of more than 600 black troops killed in this tragic accident. The *Mendi* was bisected by the empty cargo ship SS *Darro*, which was on her way to Argentina to collect a consignment of meat. The conduct of *Darro's* captain, Henry Stump, in not stopping to help the survivors, led to accusations of racism and the suspension of his captain's licence, after an investigation into the incident laid the blame squarely upon his shoulders. Batswana men had also accompanied Rhodesian troops that had been moved across the protectorate before making a famous march through the Namib Desert to remove the German presence from what is now Namibia. But for most, Batswana life went on much as before.

Perhaps the biggest impact of the Rhodesian march was that one of their number decided that he had had enough of trekking endless miles carrying a full pack, and that if he was to continue fighting he wished to do so sitting down. Arthur Harris joined the Royal Flying Corp upon his arrival in the UK and shot down five enemy aircraft, being awarded the Air Force Cross in the process. Having joined the Rhodesian Army as a bugler, he finished the war as a Major in the RAF. Although tempted to return to Africa after the armistice, he stayed with what had become the Royal Air Force, and by 1941 he was Deputy Chief of the Air Staff. The following year he would become head of Bomber Command and it was he that would mastermind the constant attack on the Third Reich from the air.

It is difficult to say why Hitler provoked a larger reaction from the Batswana chiefs than the Kaiser had. The main reasons for the response remained a loyalty to Britain and a hope that Bechuanaland would be recognised as an independent country and would not be incorporated into South Africa. These arguments had not changed since 1914. However, this time all of the chiefs, with Tshekedi Khama at their head, insisted that the Batswana would supply soldiers, but as a Bechuanaland unit and not as part of the racially divided South African military.

At first the Resident Commissioner of Bechuanaland, Charles Arden-Clarke, was more interested in forming a Home Guard to protect vital points from sabotage, especially the Bulawayo railway line and telephone wires. He also realised that Britain would no longer be in a position to subsidise the territory and that the Batswana tribes would have to pay their own way for the forthcoming years and become self-sufficient. The first practical step Arden-Clarke took was a 1940 tour of the country, explaining to the various chiefs what the situation was and asking in return for a handful of men for the Home Guard, that 'War Fields' would be grown, and that a register of men between the ages of 20 and 40 be drawn up.

By November 1940, the first thirty-five volunteers had arrived in Gaberones Village (now the capital, Gaborone), where they were issued with a uniform consisting of two bush shirts, two pairs of khaki slacks, one Askari cap and a pair of boots. Initially, the course was planned to be six weeks, but it was extended beforehand to eight in case any extra instruction was needed for 'backward pupils'. The cost of training each man to the Bechuanaland treasury was quoted as £3 for the uniform, £2 16s for rations, and £2 pocket money. These first recruits were then sent back to their villages. On their return home they were expected to start instructing their fellow villagers in basic drill and were paid a shilling a day to do so. Although the majority of these first volunteers were from the south-east of the country, there were also ten from Serowe and five from Maun in the far north-west.

The War Fields policy was intended to increase food production, but it was not a total success. Initially it was intended that the food would help feed the 4,000 members of the native forces that South Africa had raised. These Union troops were also initially used as Home Guards and were only later sent to the Middle East. At least one large field in each district would be put aside to grow crops. It was also hoped that the extra food would help raise money for the Treasury, making up for some of the lost British income. However, as the labour force dwindled when men were sent overseas, it became more difficult to tend all the fields. In addition, not all the fields were well looked after. Instead of providing the expected extra food, grain had to be imported into the country from South Africa in the period 1942 to 1947. However, many districts did provide grain from their own fields and from 1941 a war levy was introduced. Many poor Batswana were forced to sell their cattle to pay this. At the same time, extra funds were raised through gifts and donations. These totalled £13,000. The majority of this money went towards buying two Spitfires for the Royal Air Force. These Mark V machines were named *Kalahari* and *Bechuana*. The latter went into service with 317 Squadron, one of several Polish units, and it was usually flown by Zygmunt Słomski. In this aeroplane he was credited with half a Focke Wulf 190 kill and another half as a probable. Returning from a fighter sweep over France, he was hit by flak and crashed into the English Channel at the end of July 1942.

The first Spitfire donated from Bechuanaland was issued to 317 Squadron, a Polish unit serving with the RAF. (*Stanislaw Bochniak archive*)

Kalahari survived a lot longer, initially being issued to the Royal Canadian Air Force. It too participated in cross-Channel fighter sweeps aimed at keeping the Luftwaffe on its toes. Later it found its way into a Polish squadron and was being used to spot for artillery in late 1944 when it was also shot down into the Channel.

In December 1940, the chiefs had approached Arden-Clarke with a proposal to form a Bechuanaland unit for overseas service. They were particularly keen to emphasise that they wanted to fight as Batswana and not as South Africans. The British had considered plans for a joint force from the three High Commission Territories, but each time the idea had been discarded. With the loss of Crete and Greece, along with the Palestinian Pioneers, the desert war in the Middle East became crucial. This put the African Auxiliary Pioneer Corps plan back on the table. In June 1941 the derelict cold storage facility in Lobatsi, along with the land around it, was converted into a training camp. Calls went out from the chiefs for volunteers, not always a call that could be ignored. Many of the first Home Guard recruits volunteered quickly. Tshekedi Khama and his Bangwato announced the 'letsholo', a formal call to arms for his young men and a declaration of war. All over the protectorate, using donkeys, lorries, ox-carts or just feet, men congregated in their tribal capitals. Here they were sworn in and signed up, often with a thumbprint and cross, before being forwarded to Lobatsi. At the training camp they were kitted out. The light, but rugged, South African Army boots were the highlight of the new wardrobe. Here they were taught the basic drill. Many did not speak English and this was also addressed. One of the oddest problems, as recalled in Alan Bent's *Ten Thousand Men of Africa*, was the issue of what a 'right turn' meant. To Europeans that had grown up in geometrical towns and cities, 90 degrees was an obvious answer. For those who had grown up surrounded by round huts and featureless bush it just meant turning to the right, however far the recruit wished. For many other recruits this was not a problem, as they had worked in the South African mines. These ex-miners had good language skills and brought with them discipline and a knowledge of technology and machinery. They claimed that the discipline of British Army life was nothing compared with that which they had experienced in the mines.

By the end of 1941 the first seven companies had departed for Durban. Even for the miners this was a new experience, seeing the Drakensburg Mountains and, eventually, the sea for the first time. Not a single man of the first batch had ever seen a ship before and it can only be imagined what it must have been like boarding the boat for Egypt. As they left the crowded South African harbour they were serenaded by Perla Gibson, better known as the 'Lady in White'. Gibson had taken it upon herself to sing to all the warships that entered and left Durban, and by the end of the war she had completed more than 5,000 performances.

Once in Egypt they joined the British 8th Army, the most ethnically diverse fighting force the world has ever seen. Troops from every part of the Commonwealth blended together with Poles, Free French and Greeks. Soldiers from more than thirty countries swelled its ranks. Here the Batswana finished their training and each man was issued with a rifle, something unusual for African Pioneers, a tin hat, and, best of all, a greatcoat. At their training camp at Qasassin, they also experienced cinema and running hot showers for the first time. Although the British Army was de-segregated, the number of South African units serving in the Middle East meant that, even this far from home, racial politics still intruded into life for some. Several veterans never forgot the incident where black members of the South African Native Military Corps were disinterred in order that they would be buried away from their fallen white colleagues.

From Qasassin the companies were posted to where they were needed and the twenty-four units were put to a range of uses. Many found themselves in Syria, where they saw snow for the first time. Some found themselves staying in Egypt, while others were sent

Zygmunt Słomski who lost his life piloting Spitfire V *Bechuanaland* over the English Channel in 1942. (*Stanislaw Bochniak archive*)

to Palestine. One group of Batswana had a lucky escape when they watched in horror from their transports as the *Erinpura* was torpedoed. More than 600 troops from Lesotho drowned. As the war progressed several companies ended up in Italy, some via Malta. They served as heavy artillery gunners, bridge-builders, camouflage smoke-makers, drivers and mechanics, and front-line supply store shifters. The units in Italy endured the most combat as they supported the landings in Sicily and also at Reggio and Salerno. One company of smoke-makers found itself at the Battle of Monte Casino, which gained the Setswana name Marumong, or the place of bullets.

One of the original 'Bechuanaland knitters' at a remembrance lunch in 2013. (*Botswana Aviation Art*)

In all, Bechuanaland supplied twenty-four companies of men from a population of well under 500,000. This was the biggest contribution per capita of any African country and, in terms of men supplied, Bechuanaland nearly matched Uganda and Kenya, despite their joint population being more than thirty times as large. They developed a reputation for ability, courage and loyalty. In return they learned new skills and saw many new sights. Importantly, they were usually treated as equals and even mixed with white women, something unthinkable in southern Africa.

Meanwhile, back in Bechuanaland, hundreds of women were taught to knit in order to produce warm clothes, particularly hats, scarves and gloves, for those serving in colder climes thousands of miles away. The Imperial War Museum has some great pictures of this touching war effort.

RUSSIA, 1941

Even being near the coast, and the Gulf Stream that kept the waters of Murmansk largely ice free, the cold was unbearable. Servicing aeroplanes was a trial of endurance, and eventually the ground crews gave up and conceded defeat to the Arctic winter. This would be a job the Russians would pick up once the spring thaw came, and by this time Gordon Edwards would be back in the UK with a sense of a job well done.

Only two RAF squadrons were based in Russia during the Second World War, although several others would make fleeting visits. Numbers 81 and 134 Squadrons were both reformed at Leconfield in July 1941 as part of the newly created 151 Wing, created with the express purpose of helping the Russians in the fight against Operation Barbarossa, the German invasion of the Motherland.

The decision to form this Wing was essentially a political one, with the driving force coming from the very top in the form of Winston Churchill himself. Although it was difficult to see what two fighter squadrons could do against the might of the Luftwaffe, it was considered vital to show Britain's new ally that it was capable of supplying more than just kind words. The German invasion of Russia on 22 June 1941 had thrown previous alliances into chaos, with Stalin asking for immediate help from the 'capitalist imperialists' and the virulently anti-communist Churchill making a dramatic speech on the evening following the strike where he described the 'Russian soldiers standing on threshold of their native land, guarding the fields which their fathers have tilled from time immemorial'. For Stalin this was simply the calculus of survival, but it left Churchill with difficult choices to make. While the trade union movement ensured that factory workers were fully aware of the dire straits their new comrades were in, there were plenty of people who questioned the wisdom of sending material help to a country of dubious morals, especially given the still desperate situation in Britain. While conveys of supplies would take time to plan, organise and actually set sail, a couple of fighter squadrons could be mobilised quickly, couldn't they?

Just over a month after the Germans had smashed through the Russian border defences, Gordon Edwards received his new posting. Although sad to leave a battle-hardened and well recognised fighter unit in 111, there were already rumours of there being something special about 134 Squadron. For a start it was a completely new outfit, having last been disbanded before the end of the First World War. This meant that the whole squadron structure needed to be built up, almost from scratch. Gordon's proficiency rating was 'superior', and this, along with his 'very good' character, was no doubt one of the reasons for his selection. The nucleus of the new unit was formed from 'A' Flight of 17 Squadron which, ironically for Gordon, had just been sent to Scotland for a rest, having been one of the squadrons that had flown from Tangmere during the Battle of Britain. To add to the intrigue of the new arrivals, a second squadron, number 81, was also being formed at the same time, this time from 'A' Flight of 504 Squadron.

Leconfield, in the East Riding of Yorkshire, was a busy RAF station at the time with Czech and Polish fighter squadrons based there in addition to the new 151 Expeditionary Wing. With the name of the new wing offering a clue to overseas service, there was much guessing about the final destination of the RAF's newest formation. The airmen decided that the Middle East was favourite, so it was with a little shock that, after a couple of weeks, Russia leaked out as their destination. This sparked an almighty rush among all the ground crew, Gordon included. They needed to prepare for the shipping of not only the two squadrons, but also of

200 crated Hurricanes that would be reassembled and handed over
to the Russians. This was a mammoth undertaking and while the
pilots complained of having nothing to do, and enjoyed extended
leave periods, the people who actually ran a squadron worked non-
stop for the next month. Perhaps this was just as well, for only some
of the older ground crew had actually served outside of the UK,
none had been to Russia and the work gave little time for their
imaginations to kick in. For Gordon it was an extra busy time as
he was sent on two separate special instructional courses, scoring
over 80 per cent on one of these. Yet he still found time to have a
fresh medical, clearly still hoping to be a pilot one day. This time
the news was better, he was declared 'temporarily unfit for all flying
duties'. The 'temporarily' kept the dream alive and, unbeknown to
him, the words 'Recommended for Pilot Training' were added to
his service records.

When they set sail on 12 August, Gordon was lucky to be one
of the main group sent to Murmansk aboard the converted passenger liner *Llanstephan Castle*. The ship had recently taken aboard
supplies in South Africa and so had such delicacies as bacon and
oranges available. The pilots sailing behind them aboard the ancient
aircraft carrier HMS *Argus* were not quite as lucky, making do with
standard Royal Navy grub, although the claim to the daily tot of
rum would have been of some comfort.

The ground crew were the first to arrive, although they had to
wait aboard the *Castle* while a group of Russian women finished
building the dock needed to unload the ship. Time was of some
importance as the airfield at Vaenga needed to be prepared for the
arrival of the carrier-borne Hurricanes which would be flown in as
soon as the *Argus* was within range. To save any further delay, those
whose presence was required to deal with the arrival of the airborne Hurricanes were taken off the *Castle* by boat and delivered to
Vaenga. Led by the Wing's Engineering Officer, Flight Lieutenant
Gittens, the advance party was known with some amusement as the

'Erection Party'. Initially taken to a base just outside of Arkhangelsk, their first job was to unpack some of the crated Hurricanes and to prepare a radio station to contact the aircraft that would fly in from the carrier. Gordon's task here was not helped by the fact that the specialist tools needed for the Hurricane's assembly could not be found. Gittens solved this problem by working with his Russian equivalent to have new tools created from scratch. When it is considered that they did not share a common language, but only a love of engineering, the speed with which this was done was remarkable. Soon the first dozen Hurricanes were taking shape and the packing crates were used to build a shelter for the radio station. While working at Archangel, the RAF detachment was allotted an old paddle steamship as accommodation. Gordon soon found out that his lodgings were already occupied by every type of bug known to man. With his men suffering from innumerable bites, Gittens organised tents for one night while the boat was disinfected. The other problem Gordon faced was the richness of the Russian cuisine. Salmon, sausage, caviar and cabbage caused stomach problems for many of the new arrivals.

Within a week, fifteen Hurricanes had been erected and air-tested, the low cloud ensuring the local Russian population got to see their new aircraft up close. It was then time to move to Vaenga, on the outskirts of Murmansk, and join the carrier-borne Hurricanes that had just arrived.

Murmansk had already suffered severe bomb damage from the Luftwaffe and Vaenga had adapted to wartime conditions by having aircraft well dispersed and hidden in among the birch trees that surrounded the airfield. Accommodation for the airmen was very basic, though clean and warm. Running water was a problem, as there was none, but this was nothing compared with the Russian latrines. These were primitive to say the least and the smell was unbelievable. Despite these privations, by the second week of September 151 Wing was flying its first patrols, with their

One of 134 Squadron's Hurricanes at a muddy Vaenga before the snows arrived.
(*Mark Sheppard Collection*)

Hurricanes wearing a mix of RAF letters and Russian bort numbers. Number 81 Squadron claimed the Wing's first kills on the twelfth, shooting down a pair of Messerschmitts, but at the cost of one of its own pilots: Sergeant Smith was killed while trying to make a forced landing in his shot-up Hurricane. The damage had included the guide rail for the canopy, meaning that he had been trapped in his aircraft and was unable to bail out.

The Russians, impressed with their new allies' success, insisted that each RAF pilot that made a kill was awarded the 1,000-rouble prize available to the local pilots. A compromise was agreed, whereby the money gained would be paid into the RAF Benevolent Fund.

Number 81 Squadron continued to have success in battles against the Luftwaffe, while Gordon's 134 Squadron never seemed to find the Germans in the air. Number 134 were also tasked with converting Russian pilots to the Hurricane. The first to take to the air was the local commander, Major General Kuznetsov. He had formed a good relationship with the RAF Wing Commander in charge of 151 Wing, the wonderfully named New Zealander, Henry Neville Gynes Ramsbottom-Isherwood. The Russian had already made several visits to Vaenga and had done everything he could to help the British contingent. On these trips he had often brought an ex-schoolmistress with him and she had translated the cockpit drill and pilot's notes. With a Hurricane specially marked for the occasion, Kuznetsov took off and did a series of touch and goes before coming in for a perfect three-point landing.

Gordon's job now was a mixture of keeping the Hurricanes airborne and passing his expertise onto his Russian colleagues. As the weather headed towards winter, this job became more and more difficult as 134's dispersal area started to become waterlogged. This made working on the aircraft when they were stationary unpleasant, but it had further implications for operations. To taxi through the mud and up the slope to the runway, the Hurricane needed a lot of power. To stop the aircraft from nosing over, two airmen would be given the job of lying across the back end of the aeroplane. Usually this procedure just led to cold, wet, dirty and bedraggled ground crew, but on one occasion it led to tragedy. Vic Berg was scrambled to meet an incoming raid on 27 September and he took off with the two airmen still clinging onto the rear of his Hurricane. The extra weight sent the aircraft's nose high into the Arctic sky before the Hurricane fell back to earth from a height of 50 feet. Both of Gordon's comrades were killed instantly while Berg ended up in hospital in Murmansk with serious leg injuries. Fortunately, this incident marked the last fatalities suffered by the Wing while in Russia.

On 6 October, in the last big air battle, 134 Squadron finally claimed success. A large force of Ju 88s, attacking from Norway, was intercepted by both squadrons and at least two of the bombers fell to 134 pilot's guns. This action really marked the end of the fighting for 151 Wing as the winter started to close in. The weather was not the only reason for the end of RAF operations. As 134 trained more pilots and ground crew, it was time for 81 Squadron to start handing over its aircraft to the Russians. By 22 October the surviving thirty-six Hurricanes of 151 Wing had all been transferred to the newly formed 'No. 1 Hurricane Squadron'. This marked the end of operations for the RAF pilots, but for Gordon and the ground crew, life went on pretty much as before as they instructed their Russian equivalents on how to assemble the remaining crated Hurricanes. This was not just practical advice as Gittens also organised technical exams for his Soviet pupils.

Increasingly heavy snow put an end to almost all flying and the grounded RAF pilots started to make their own entertainment. When severe injuries were incurred on a powered sledging outing, Ramsbottom-Isherwood devised a daily plan of physical training, including brutal route marches, for his bored officers and men. Eventually, the weather put paid to these as well. Another factor that affected everyone was the lack of daylight, Murmansk being so far north that in November a dim twilight was as bright as it got. At the end of that month, after a lavish party, 151 Wing returned by ship to the UK. Gordon thought that the return trip was much worse as the fog and ice often reduced speed to 5 knots and the navy ships lacked the comforts of the *Llanstephan Castle*.

No. 151 Wing left Russia with the proud record of not only delivering 200 aircraft and training Russian pilots and ground crew in their use, but of shooting down fifteen German aircraft for the loss of only one Hurricane – raising £300 for the Benevolent fund in the process. They also left with four Orders of Lenin awarded to its members, the only ones to be given to non-Russians during the conflict. Gordon Edwards returned to the UK a truly battle-hardened 'erk', with knowledge of a little Russian and, more importantly, of how to keep aeroplanes in the air in the harshest conditions.

BECHUANALAND, 1941

What is a Bushman? Most of our local pundits disagree profoundly.

The above note, scribbled over the minutes of a meeting to discuss the 'Bushman Issue' in the protectorate in 1937, encapsulates the confusion around Bushmen that has lasted until today. A government study of Bushmen had been planned, but by 1941 it had been shelved, incomplete and unread. As the various chiefs urged their young men to join up and fight far away, the leaderless people not affiliated to the Batswana went about life as normal, almost unnoticed.

Even 2,000 years earlier, before the arrival of black Bantu-speaking people, there was no simple answer to the government official's question. There was not a single integrated band of 'Bushmen', but instead different groups with different dialects and lifestyles. These dialects, largely based on the famous clicking Khoisan, had diverged enough to be recognised as different languages. At least six separate linguistic families had developed in the lands that were to become Botswana. Lifestyles depended on where these Stone-Age people lived, some depending on wild food, some hunting, while those by the northern rivers fished. All were skilled makers of stone tools and they traded between different groups. Generally, they were short people with light brown, rather than black, skin and distinctive high cheek bones.

The size of settlements depended on these lifestyles, some being permanent while other groups seemed more willing to move to where food was easier to find. As mentioned earlier, there is evidence that by this time some villages owned cattle and grew crops. Some groups of Bushmen have words for cows and goats that are linguistically distinct from later Bantu languages, suggesting ancient origins. Pottery arrived in this part of Africa at the same time as domesticated animals, suggesting trade with people from East Africa. The animals hunted, and even the fish caught, by these people can be deduced from the numerous surviving rock paintings.

The first wave of Bantu migration seems to have had little effect on the original inhabitants, although intermarriage seems to have been common. This meant that some groups, such as the Deti, living on the Boteti River, and the Xani, living in the Okavango Delta, became largely genetically Bantu yet kept a Khoi-based language and their traditional lifestyle. Other groups mixed to a lesser extent, but the way that cultures and religious ideas merged suggest that none were completely untouched.

With the expansion of Tswana-speaking people in the middle of the second millennium, pressure was put onto the original inhabitants of what was to become Botswana. Some were pushed further into the Kalahari, while others lost their land and cattle to the newcomers. The Batswana generally did not consider the people they found to be their equals and they incorporated them into the lowest strata of their society. They were considered property and were used for menial tasks and cattle herding. However, some groups with strong headmen or chiefs, such as the Deti, maintained some independence and others, such as the Zhu and Tyua, put up armed resistance. Some Bushmen traded with the Batswana and acted as hunters and guides. Their legendary tracking skills were already widely appreciated; one of the lesser known of these skills was the ability to track 'honey-guides'. These dull brown little birds would be followed until the hives, with their valuable honey, were discovered. However, many of these relationships seem to have become increasingly one-sided.

As time went by, the Batswana groups became stronger and, after they armed and regrouped following the *Difaqane*, more and more Bushmen found themselves under the rule of local Batswana chiefs. By the end of the nineteenth century there were no longer any powerful groups of independent Bushmen left. Only those in country so harsh or so infested by Tsetse fly that cattle raising was impossible carried on living as before.

Life under Batswana rule could be very hard with no rights and regular beatings. Children were often considered to be the property of the family their parents worked for. Even Khama III, known as 'Khama the Good', made only limited improvements to the lives of his Basarwa. Under LMS pressure, Bushmen were accepted into the church. The Reverend James Hepburn, who spent years with the Bangwato, wrote of his pleasure that the Basarwa were now buried by their 'masters', although he still faced arguments from some leading Batswana in his church who felt that 'Bushmen were no better than animals, dogs with no souls'. While Khama encouraged the payment, in goats or cattle, for those Basarwa who worked for Bangwato families, this was by no means universally accepted.

While waiting for Khama's grandson, Seretse, to come of age, Tshekedi Khama took charge of the Bangwato. Tshekedi was another forward-looking member of the Khama dynasty and had been behind the construction of the first airfield in Botswana in 1922. This was nominated as one of the stopping points of the first Cairo to Cape air race, bringing unrivalled excitement to those lucky enough to see cutting-edge technology fly over the mud hut village.

Tshekedi introduced primary schools, grain silos and even a college in Serowe, but the British invested little in infrastructure and with no tarred roads the only efficient transport was the Rhodesian railway. At the same time the chiefs, including Tshekedi, blocked suggestions for developing mining interests due to the fear that this would bring European settlers and lead to proper colonisation. The introduction of a 'Hut Tax' meant that by the 1920s a significant number of Batswana earned cash by working in the South African mines and the chiefs had no interest in seeing the same exploitation within in their own country.

The arrival of a new Resident Commissioner in 1929 was to seriously put the cat among the pigeons. Charles Rey was appointed to

develop what the Dominions Office felt was a territory that was drifting under previously weak administration. Rey was a paternalist in
the best traditions of Empire. Like all fathers he could be authoritarian and he believed he knew what was best for his 'children'. Sadly his
own two sons had died very young of dysentery while he was working for the Abyssinian Company in Addis Ababa, a tragedy his wife,
Ninon, never really recovered from. Rey did not suffer fools gladly,
especially within the white community at Mafeking, but he did have
a sense of humour that seems to have been delivered with a twinkle in
his eye. He referred to one colonial official as having 'all the backbone
of a filleted sole'. He also had a dislike of 'brainless' missionaries, who
he considered to be troublemakers, and he also had a strange habit
of substituting the word 'cucumber' for the more accurate 'concubine'.
His car, *Topsy*, was a common sight on the dusty, sandy, rutted tracks
around Mafeking and the southern parts of the protectorate, either
on official business or just on a picnic with Ninon.

Resident Commissioner Charles Rey (left) with his wife (centre), along with
Robert and Phyllis Reilly. (*John Reilly Collection*)

Within months of taking up the post, he had to deal with Basarwa issues. The first involved reprimanding Tshekedi for sending men into another chief's territory to bring back some Basarwa that had run away. He made it clear that Bushmen were not slaves and could live where they wanted. Another Bushman asked to pay his Hut Tax in order to show his Batswana chief that he was 'a man, not a dog'. He said the chief's people would rob him, taking the skins he had collected, but he hoped the receipt for the Hut Tax would show that the British Government regarded him as a man. In January 1931, Rey had to deal with the murder of a Basarwa man by the group sent to recapture him. Once again it was Tshekedi Khama's Bangwato involved. It was clear that the Bushmen were considered as slaves, not people or even serfs. The murdered man had more than 300 wounds on his body. Rey was furious when the murderers escaped the death penalty on a legal technicality. These incidents led to an official from England undertaking an investigation into the conditions, particularly with regards to slavery, of the Bushmen in Tshekedi's fiefdom. This report was published in South Africa in 1933 and was meant to have led to a larger inquiry that was never completed.

In his diaries, Rey described a Bangwato cattle post herded by Basarwa. The Bushmen's 'bones were sticking out' and they were 'too cowed and dejected to take an interest in anything' having being nearly starved to death. The herders were not paid, except in milk from the cows, and had to scavenge for roots and berries to supplement this. Rey shot a springbok and gave it to them, watching them set upon it 'like a pack of starving wolves' while he stood over them, making sure their Bangwato masters did not interfere.

Incidents like this meant that Rey had little respect for Tshekedi Khama, whom he held responsible for the treatment of the people under his jurisdiction. Despite his own authoritarian streak, Rey had a firm belief in the equality of man and had little time for the racial policies being enacted in South Africa. He seems to have had a genuine concern for the local population. He worried that they were not always well served by their chiefs, some of whom he considered to be 'autocratic, half-educated, and to some extent, thoroughly rotten'. Tshekedi Khama was also a strong personality and not one to let go of grudges. Following an attempted shooting, he had expelled two men from Serowe and confiscated their property. When he was found to have acted illegally, Tshekedi took his case all the way to the Privy Council, against Rey's advice. The most serious case of Tshekedi and Rey locking horns was over the 'McIntosh Incident' which caused the deployment of a Royal Naval detachment to the edge of the Kalahari, nearly 1,000 miles inland.

Phinehas Macintosh was a white trader in Serowe with a bad reputation for an alcohol-fuelled interest in native girls. During one dispute he struck a black rival in an argument over a particular girl. Under the law of the land, Europeans were only to be tried by the British administration, local chiefs being barred from administering justice to white men. Claiming that previous complaints against McIntosh had been ignored, Tshekedi Khama took matters into his own hands and had the trader flogged. Rey, who was already developing plans to reduce the chief's powers, was not amused. Having recently had problems with a headman where policemen had been manhandled, Rey decided that a show of force was required if action was to be taken against Tshekedi. Given that the whole administration of the protectorate numbered less than 300 men, only forty of whom were non-native, Rey decided to send for reinforcements. One hundred and sixty-five marines were boarded onto a train on the South African coast, complete with field guns. That, Rey felt, would be more than enough to deal with the 'poisonous little rat'.

Tshekedi was summoned from Serowe to the racecourse at Palapye where he claimed that he had the authority to try who he wanted. The response from the British was to suspend his chieftainship and banish him to Francistown. This was done in front of the arrayed marines. The Bangwato refused to elect another chief and Rey was accused by some in London of acting with excessive force. Eventually both men backed down, and, after an apology, Tshekedi was reinstated.

Rey was very keen to modernise the protectorate and he had many schemes to do this. He worked hard to increase the export of cattle, overcoming South African obstacles and opening new trade routes to the north. He developed cold stores and creameries in Francistown and Lobatsi. These were part of a scheme to encourage native production and export of butter. He had grand plans for a trans-Kalahari railway, both to open up new business and also to by-pass South Africa. Under his rule the first regular air services into and around the protectorate were initiated, including flights from Johannesburg to Maun. Twice the protectorate won first place at trade shows in Johannesburg; the second time the impressive display included fresh produce flown in from Bechuanaland. A national radio station was set up and run. He was also interested in getting mines into the areas Tshekedi had banned them from.

A combination of meeting these aims and improving the lives of the common people led Rey to look at how the Batswana chiefs' powers could be reduced. Up until this point, the chiefs had been left to rule their territories with minimal interference and oversight. Rey wanted to introduce an element of democracy to the tribal system by setting up tribal councils, chosen by the *kgotla* or village meeting, to assist chiefs in their rule. The chiefs could only rule with the approval of the council and the British, otherwise they risked being removed. New law courts would be set up. These would still be run by headmen and chiefs, but records had to be kept and decisions could now be appealed to the British District Commissioner. While Rey saw these as protecting the people, many others saw it as an assault on Batswana tradition and custom. Tshekedi saw it as a direct assault on his power and led the chiefs against these 'Native Proclamations'. Tshekedi failed initially and they were implemented in 1934. Two years of legal challenges followed, but the proclamations stood even though they were not always followed. Throughout his battles with Rey, Tshekedi made very good use of the media, often using the London Missionary Society to get his side of the story to London quicker than it was possible through Rey's official channels. By the time Rey left in 1937, Bechuanaland had developed quicker than in any other period of its history and, through his successes and failures, it was well and truly on the map.

Rey's successor, Charles Arden-Clarke, saw the territory return to drifting along. Many of Rey's schemes went unfinished or were left unused. The cold house at Lobatsi fell into disrepair and the radio station was closed down. Arden-Clarke did work with the chiefs to make the proclamations more acceptable to them, meaning a return to more centralised power in the hands of the chiefs. In return, Arden-Clarke made a promise that the protectorate would not be handed over to South Africa. In addition, he set up Botswana's first Board of Education. With hindsight, these were some of the reasons that by the start of the war the chiefs were still pro-British.

EGYPT, 1942

They sent us out to Egypt
A very pleasant land
Where miles and miles of sweet FA
Are covered up with sand

Gordon Edwards could hardly have helped but to sing along with the latest ditty doing the rounds. He had followed 134 Squadron out to the land of the pharaohs only to find that there were no aeroplanes for the squadron to fly. Another gremlin in the service system.

No. 134 Squadron had returned from Russia, having handed over their Hurricanes to the Russian Navy, and had re-equipped at RAF Catterick, next to the Great North Road in North Yorkshire. This was the second time Gordon had seen his pilots trade in Hurricanes for the much sexier Spitfires. A few pilots still claimed to miss the sturdy Hawker aircraft, but most saw their time in Russia as deserving of the new sleeker aeroplanes. To the ground crew it made little difference, but being part of a Spitfire squadron had a certain gloss when visiting the local pubs on a Saturday night. Even the north-eastern weather could not spoil Christmas 1941.

As soon as the squadron was comfortable on the new mounts they were moved again, this time to Northern Ireland. This had the benefit, from the mechanics' point of view, of little chance of action, not to mention noticeably more farm produce on the mess tables. The pilots no doubt resented being far away from the action, and they cannot have been pleased when some of their new Spitfires were replaced by battle-weary Hurricanes. However, the whole squadron had perked up at the news of a posting to warmer climes.

Once again Gordon found himself on a passenger liner, this time bound for Egypt. Due to the situation in the Mediterranean, this meant a very long trip around the Cape of Good Hope. This did have the benefit of a few stolen nights ashore in South Africa, at this time of the year colder than most of the RAF members would have believed. The weather was not on the minds of many who got off the boat, though. It is not known how many fatherless children were left in the ports of Cape Town and Durban. Perhaps the effects of a lively society far away from the troubles in Europe on men who had not seen a city lit up at night for nearly three years can be understood. After a very good time, the RAF personnel had now to leave and sail on to Egypt. As they left the harbour in Durban they passed the lady in white, singing through her megaphone to comfort every leaving ship.

Upon arrival in Egypt, Gordon found himself with his squadron at RAF Kasfareet on the banks of the Suez Canal, but of the expected Hurricanes there was no sign. After a short delay the Middle East Command decided that the pilots should be sent to other operational units and that the ground crew was to be used as a servicing squadron. Kasfareet was a well equipped base with few of the problems that faced front-line bases. It had a good water supply and its own cinema with daily showings. In 1942 these included such hits as *Too Hot to Handle* with Clarke Gable, *Miss Fix It* headed by Jane Withers and Gloria Stuart, and the unmissable *Young Dr Kildare*. However, it was still very hot and flies were a constant source of annoyance. Several airmen kept pet chameleons that were not only cute and exotic, but, as one airman put it, 'very useful for picking flies off your stomach as you lay on your bed'.

By the time Gordon had settled in, the Middle East had seen battles rage back and forth along the northern coast of Africa for nearly a year and a half. Italy's entry to the war in mid-1940 had seen numerous small-scale skirmishes with British forces based in Egypt. However, August 1940 saw the Italians make a serious push into Egypt under Marshal Graziani that was only ended when his

Gordon Edwards (right) enjoys an off-duty stroll around Kasfareet. (*Edwards family*)

logistical supplies became stretched. The British, along with Indian and Australian troops, counter-attacked in December, advancing hundreds of miles and capturing 130,000 Italian troops. This led Anthony Eden to quip, 'Never has so much been surrendered by so many to so few.' This assault and counter-assault, combined with stretched supply lines, set the pattern for the conflict.

While the British lost much equipment and many valuable men in the battles for Greece and Crete, the Germans came to the rescue of their Italian allies in Libya with the formation of the Afrika Korps under the brilliant Erwin Rommel. The charismatic German soon won back the ground Graziani had lost, with only the port city of Tobruk offering unwavering resistance. The formation of the British Eighth Army in September 1941 under Lieutenant-General Alan Cunningham saw the creation of the most diverse fighting force the world had ever seen, with soldiers from more than thirty countries among its ranks. This amalgamation of so many diverse forces soon proved its worth, pushing Rommel back and lifting the siege of Tobruk. This was the situation when Gordon arrived in Egypt.

In June 1942, with the British in the process of preparing an offensive, Rommel struck and pushed the Eighth Army back to El Alamein, deep within Egyptian territory. Having already gone through several commanders, General William Gott was given the job of leading the Eighth's latest counter-attack. Unfortunately, before he could take up his post the lumbering Bristol Bombay transport he was flying in was shot down by Bf 109s of Jagdgeschwader 27. Even though the pilot had made a good forced landing, the German pilots strafed the crashed aeroplane, killing all those still inside. This apparent disaster led to the appointment of Lieutenant-General Bernard Montgomery who patiently prepared his forces for what many would later consider the turning point of the war. The second Battle of Alamein in October 1942 was the beginning of an offensive that would eventually drive Axis forces from the African continent. As Montgomery pushed westward,

Operation Torch landed Allied troops in Tunisia, meaning that Rommel was caught in a huge pincer movement.

With the creation of the Desert Air Force (DAF), the Royal Air Force played a significant role in these victories. Similar to the Eighth Army, the nominally British DAF was a diverse group, with squadrons from many countries. South Africa in total provided more than a dozen squadrons, roughly a third of the force's total strength at any one time. Gordon's entrance on the scene coincided with a rapid expansion of the DAF. The twelve months from October 1941 saw the number of flying units expand from sixteen to twenty-nine squadrons. This period also saw an improvement in equipment, including the arrival of the first Spitfires to the region. This meant that for the first time the DAF had fighters that could match the Luftwaffe's Messerschmitts in air combat. Until that point, the use of obsolete aircraft had meant the DAF had suffered high losses, unable to out-fly, out-climb or out-pace the Bf 109s of Jadgdeschwader 27. Pilots did have much better luck against the often biplane-equipped Italians.

However, Gordon was well aware that the Germans and Italians were by no means the biggest danger to aircrew. To force-land in the desert was often a death sentence, and a particularly unpleasant one at that. Surrounded by hundreds of miles of hostile terrain, some of the driest and harshest on the planet, it was a lucky pilot indeed that was rescued. Often it was only mummified remains and desperate last words that were found. The case of Sergeant Mikolajczak was one that stuck in Gordon's mind. A Polish pilot who had been forced to land his fighter due to mechanical failure, he had left notes detailing his final painful hours. Knowing that he was dying, he had a chance to say goodbye to his family and his beloved Poland. He had tried to walk out of the desert but, when he had gone as far as he physically could, he had been forced to return to his grounded aircraft, eight hours of energy wasted walking through featureless desert. The last two entries provide a haunting reminder of the dangers of the Sahara:

Time 1200 hours, 10th May. It is terribly hot, I drink, or rather I lick my scanty sweat. I am suffering terribly.
1345 hours – I hear an aircraft flying to the south my right, my last hope, I cannot get up to have a look. My last minutes. God have mercy on me.

The Desert Air Force provided vital air support to the troops on the ground, a role suited to P-40 Kittyhawks and to specialist aircraft like the tank-busting Hurricane Mk.IID. This version of the tried and trusted Hawker aeroplane was equipped with two massive 40mm cannon that devastated Axis vehicles, even heavily armoured Panzers. No. 6 Squadron earned the nickname 'The Tin Openers' flying these machines. The DAF pioneered the role of the Forward Air Controller, embedding RAF personnel in Army units to direct air attacks via radio. This tactic was combined with the use of 'cab ranks' of fighter-bombers that would orbit in the air until called into action.

The fact that the battle for North Africa swung back and forth so much meant that considerable equipment was captured. This ranged from the acquirement of thousands of precious jerry cans, which

Captured, but wrecked, German Me 109s of Jagdgeschwader 27 at El Daba. (*Staff Sergeant George O'Neill*)

A rare sight in the desert, a Dornier Do-24. (*Staff Sergeant George O'Neill*)

A Ju-87 Stuka at El Daba. (*Staff Sergeant George O'Neill*)

were much better designed than their British equivalents, to the securing of entire aircraft. South African Staff Sergeant George O'Neill was one of those involved in the recovery of German aircraft from overrun airfields, as well as those shot down. His photo album shows captured Bf 109 fighters, Stuka dive bombers, Gotha Go 242 gliders, and even a Dornier Do 24 flying boat that was literally grounded in the desert. It was not just those on the ground that were involved in these recoveries, as highlighted by the case of the 'Stolen Stuka'. After a squadron of Italian Ju 87 Stukas had apparently made forced landings in the desert, Wing Commander Bowman and Squadron Leader Rozier were sent out to try and fly one back for evaluation purposes. After two days of adventure, they returned to base with their prize, complete with a naval officer in the gunner's position. The latter, a destroyer commander, had decided to spend his leave in the desert 'having a look around'!

For more mundane aeroplanes, the RAF had several aircraft recovery sections that would go out into the desert to retrieve downed aircraft so they could either be returned to service or stripped for spares. These units were equipped with Bedford 'Queen Mary' transporters that could carry most aircraft once their wings had been removed, these being stored lengthwise on the lorry, alongside the fuselage. These trips into the desert were not risk free and were often given either Army or RAF Regiment escorts. The difficult terrain and extensive use of minefields by both sides made their task difficult enough without the chance of coming across an enemy patrol. The recovered airframes were returned to Maintenance Units where aircraftmen like Gordon would assess their condition before making a decision on whether they could be returned to the air. It is possible that Gordon came across Batswana troops here for the first time as several dozen of the volunteers from Bechuanaland worked in aircraft recovery sections, either as mechanics or drivers.

In addition to repairing downed aircraft, the usual task of maintaining those in squadron service had to be continued. Much work was done on their home airfields, but for more serious repairs or overhauls these aircraft too would be sent to the Maintenance Units. Occasionally damaged aircraft would be flown to these units to be repaired. This was the case of the P-40 flown by Flight Sergeant Dennis Copping. The Kittyhawk took off for the Maintenance Unit in June 1942 with an unserviceable compass one of the items on the list to be repaired. That was the last the world saw of the 24-year-old pilot. Seventy years later a Polish oil worker found his perfectly preserved aeroplane in the Libyan Desert. It appeared that Copping set off to walk, but, with the nearest town 200 miles away, it was an impossible task. The desert had claimed another victim.

Eventually 134's new Hurricanes arrived in Egypt, only seven months after the rest of the squadron. This meant that most of the ground crew were reunited with their unit. However, Gordon had by this time moved on. Bored by Egypt, and not having a real squadron to work with, he had reapplied for pilot training and this time, having passed his medical at last, had been accepted. This would be a chance to realise his dreams.

His old colleagues would spend nearly another year ranging along the North African coast as the battle swayed, but now mainly one way, along the narrow strip of land that stretched from Egypt in the west to Tunisia in the east. This included the capture of Tripoli and the eventual surrender of Axis forces. As the action in the Middle East petered out, 134 was posted to India, still flying its trusted Hawker aircraft. They would spend the final two years of the conflict fighting the Japanese, in India and also Burma, in what would become known as 'the forgotten war'. They were one of the last Hurricane operators, eventually trading their weary cannon-equipped, canvas-tailed fighters in for the massive American-built Republic P-47 Thunderbolts in August 1944. In June 1945 the squadron was renumbered 131 County of Kent, after the original 131 had handed over its Spitfires to the Indian Air Force. In December that year the squadron was disbanded for good.

BECHUANALAND, 1943

The sun was low in the sky, aided by the dust in the air in painting the whole environment a delicate pink. Several impala edged their way towards the watering hole as the heat of the day started at last to dissipate. Bang! One of the antelope tottered and fell. Twai Twai Molele's family would eat well that night.

The use of rifles for hunting had largely replaced the traditional methods for many of the Bushmen who had been in contact with either the Tswana tribes or with travelling Europeans. Only those deep in the Kalahari Desert still relied exclusively on the knowledge of plants and animal behaviour for hunting. The first missionaries and European hunters had been both fascinated and impressed by the skill of these strange little people and left detailed accounts. The most memorable descriptions recalled endurance hunting.

Also known as persistence hunting, this involves a group of hunters tracking and chasing down prey over a number of hours during the hottest part of the day. While not quick enough to catch many large animals in Botswana, a human can develop enough endurance to overcome this handicap. By repeatedly forcing an animal to run and then tracking it down before it has time to recover properly, it can be exhausted to the point where it can run no more. The Bushmen are aided by the fact the humans can sweat much more than their prey and so can keep cooler, and of course they can carry water with them. A kudu hunt might last eight hours from initially finding the antelope to finally despatching it with a thankful prayer and a spear. Temperatures during these hunts could easily exceed 40°C.

The alternative to a marathon in scorching temperatures was to use poisoned arrows. The San of the central Kalahari were already famous for their hunting technique, using skilful and silent tracking to get in such a position to launch an arrow tipped with a venom powerful enough to bring down the largest animal. Because of the exceptionally light nature of the bows and arrows used, the initial injury was almost always insufficient to be fatal so the choice of an effective poison was important.

In the western Kalahari, the milky sap from *Euphorbia viros*, a cactus-like tree also known as the Gifboom, was used. In the northern part of the desert, including the Nata region, *Diamphidia Nigroornata* was used. This beetle, which bears a passing resemblance to a ladybird, lays its eggs on *Commiphora* plants. The larvae then feast on the leaves before burying themselves in a cocoon a few millimetres below the sandy surface where it will wait, for several years if necessary, for the perfect conditions to emerge.

The San would collect these larvae and either squeeze them directly onto their arrows, not at the tips – to avoid accidents – or make a paste using plant juices and other ingredients such as scorpions' tails and spiders, and apply this to the arrow shaft. Despite these careful preparations, this poison could take several hours to bring down a beast, even days in the case of a giraffe. This meant that the tracking skills were again needed, for an injured animal might still walk tens of kilometres.

Whichever method was used for a particular hunt, care had to be taken by the hunting party as the bush held many dangers. Snakes were an ever present threat, but would largely mind their own business. However, larger animals might have taken a close interest in the hunt and it was not unknown for a pride of lions or a pack of hyenas to make off with the kill, leaving a hungry, tired and helpless hunting party empty-handed.

Twai Twai Molele was well aware of the many different poisons that could be used to tip arrows, for he was an experienced herbalist. He was what the missionaries would call a witch doctor, using the term out of both ignorance and as a way to deter their converts from visiting such people.

The Tyua group to which he belonged shared many of their beliefs with the Khoisan to whom they were related. The world had been made by a god that was responsible for the creation of the earth, the plants, the animals and the weather. This god had both male and female forms. Originally all creatures could talk, but when man sinned animals were turned into men and men to animals, losing the ability to speak. The belief of this close relationship between men and animals led to the longstanding tradition of only killing animals when necessary, otherwise their god would be angry, and food and rain would dry up. As well as this creator god, a 'trickster' god existed to try and undo the good work of the creator. This trickster lived among people and controlled their lives, bringing joy and sadness, health and sickness. People would ask the creator god for good health and rain, but would turn to the trickster when they were in trouble. Medicine men such as Twai Twai would provide a conduit to these gods.

Dance played an important part in these dealings with the gods and spirits. Around a campfire in the cold evening air, to the accompaniment of staccato clapping, songs that could tell of healing, happiness or fighting evil spirits would be sung while the men danced. Often these dances would go on for hours with their participants entering a trance-like state where people would be imbued with animal spirits, allowing communication with the gods. Occasionally dances would go on throughout the night, leaving those involved in a state of exhaustion. In the silence of the bush, the sounds of such a gathering could easily travel 20 miles. A darker side to this spiritualism was the belief that certain body parts could bring power to their new owners. Ritual murder was certainly common in the north-east of Botswana, with male genitals believed to bring especially good luck. In the 1960s a case in Tsamaya, a tiny village on the Bulawayo railway line between Francistown and the Rhodesian border, led to the discovery of more than twenty victims. The unlucky men, for the majority of the killed were male, were often poisoned by a group of women before being dispatched. Their private parts would then be buried in fields to ensure a good crop for that season. This 'coven' had apparently acted under the orders of a local headman and the murders had been carried out over a number of decades.

Twai Twai Molele had been born in the last decade of the previous century near the Rhodesian border, further upstream along the Nata River. The Tyua group that he belonged to was unusual in that they had a significant number of Bantu ancestors, as shown by modern blood and DNA testing. Yet their Shua language was undoubtedly part of the San 'click' family of speech and they were definitely considered 'Bushmen'. This term would have been applied partly because of their semi-nomadic lifestyle, combining settled life during the wet season with hunting over a wide area as food literally dried up during the late dry season from July to October.

The Nata River runs in a south-westerly direction through sandy soil that supports the usual low acacia bush with occasional taller trees in areas that retain moisture. The sand is sometimes several hundred metres thick and from the air it is almost possible to pick out the gentle dunes that exist underneath the scrub. For most of the year the river is dry, but once the rains arrive in October flash floods can fill it to spilling point, turning the surrounding sand and dust into a series of muddy puddles and tributaries. Like the more famous Okavango, the Nata River empties not into the sea, but instead into a large inland delta.

Originally this fed Lake Makgadikgadi, a huge inland sea, but when this dried up several thousand years ago it left more than 6,000 square miles of barren salt plains. To give an idea of scale, these salt pans have a total area roughly double that of North Yorkshire, the largest British county. The Nata River supplies a shallow lake around its mouth that fills only a fraction of the Makgadikgadi to a depth of inches rather than feet. This provides a home to thousands of flamingos as well as many other bird types. During the rainy season, the new grass that springs up around the pans attracts herbivores such as zebra and wildebeest from farther afield, along with their predators. During the early part of the twentieth century giraffe were common in the Nata area, but elephants had already been hunted to such an extent that they sought refuge northwards, towards the forests that lined the Chobe River.

Massive and ancient baobab trees provided useful landmarks in this otherwise featureless landscape. The nineteenth-century artist Thomas Baines painted a group of seven of these mighty trees in the pans during one of his expeditions in the region. Today these are known as Baines' Baobabs and are thought to be 4,000 years old. Another famous home to baobabs is Kubu Island, a rocky outpost in the middle of the dry flats of the Makgaikgadi. One of these trees in the Nata region served as an unofficial post office with messages left on its bark, while a hollow baobab in Kasane was used as a prison, complete with a solid lockable door.

Up until the time of Twai Twai's birth, the Tyua had been independent under leaders such as Kgaraxumae who had fought for at least a generation against the encroaching Bangwato under

Since hunted to the point of extinction, Twai Twai would have been aware of the dangers posed by rhinoceroses, especially those with young. (*Joanna Poweska*)

A collection of baobabs at Kubu Island in the middle of the Makgadikgadi Pans. These mighty trees have been used as landmarks, a post office and even a prison. (*Joanna Poweska*)

Khama III. Trade with neighbouring people was brisk, including with the Bangwato, although some Tyua would hang around cattle posts seeking odd jobs in return for payment. However, by the mid-1890s, Khama's men had effectively enslaved the Tyua and they were relegated to menial tasks like many of the other San people before them. The Molele family were not easy to control, however. In 1898 a group of migrant Zambian workers were making their way home when they disappeared. Although their remains were not found for some time and little proof of their supposed murder was gathered, it was considered common knowledge in the region that the Molele family had been involved in the robbing and subsequent killing of the unfortunate travellers. It must be remembered, however, that this was naturally dangerous territory to walk through even if well armed. Indeed, it was still common practice during Twai Twai's childhood for many Tyua to sleep in the trees, lions being considered such a

deadly threat, especially at night. It is, however, interesting to note
that when anthropologist Richard Lee lived with the !Kung bushmen of the western Kalahari during the 1960s, he did some research
into murder rates among these supposedly peaceful people. He had
chosen the !Kung because they had had probably the least interac-
tion with external peoples and lived a traditional hunter-gatherer
lifestyle. In contrast to the romantic 'living in perfect harmony' image
promoted by writers such as Laurens van der Post, he discovered that
murder was about three times more prevalent than in the United
States. Infanticide was also frequent, especially in the case of twins
which were considered evil.

Twai Twai grew into an impressive young man, tall even by
European standards, and he would have stood out as a powerful
example of manhood among the traditionally short Bushmen; evi-
dently his Bantu bloodline was strong. If his appearance alone was
not sufficient to attract women and intimidate competitors, then
his growing knowledge of medicine and spiritualism gave him an
extra edge.

Twai Twai certainly seems to have had a powerful influence over
the opposite sex. He took several wives and had children with other
women too. It was rumoured that one of his conquests came at the
cost of her husband's life, but again local gossip never translated into
proof or an arrest. The complicated family tree that emerged from
his various liaisons was perhaps not unique. Certainly, polygamy
was still common and the idea of an extended family group was cul-
turally accepted. His growing notoriety and strong personality did
put him in direct conflict with Khama's district overseer, who went
by the name of Oitsile. The overseer's job was to ensure that Khama's
interests in the Nata area were well served, seeing that fields were
tended and cattle herded. The Molele family were supposed to look
after many heads of cattle for Khama. These cows would spend the
days wandering freely through the bush only with the protection of
a herd-boy, despite the threat from lions. Tensions between the two

men had gradually built up before Oitsile was accused of murdering Twai Twai's pregnant teenage daughter. Oitsile was lucky to escape a lynching, while Twai Twai was forced to leave his village and he was driven to live as something of a Robin Hood figure in the bush.

For sixteen years Twai Twai lived as a bandit, building a growing reputation for strength, something many put down to witchcraft – a rumour that he did nothing to restrain. Eventually a compromise was reached with Tshekedi Khama and Twai Twai was encouraged to settle in Nekate, a tiny village a few miles outside of Nata. Here he promised to look after a new batch of cattle, Tshekedi clearly hoping that this would keep him out of trouble. This worked to a limited extent, with Twai Twai settling down with his latest wife and daughter, Rekisang.

This period of calm did not last long as Twai Twai developed a reputation for not taking good care of the cattle under his charge. One reason for this was that as food ran short, with the final April rains fading in the memory, Twai Twai would organise illegal hunting parties. These would consist of perhaps five to ten men from his extended family along with a handful of young girls and women. They would disappear into the wild for maybe a month, leaving the fields and cattle unattended, and seek out meat from the large variety of animals that still roamed the bush in the Crown lands to the north of Nata. These animals included a wide range of antelope ranging from small duiker to the impressive kudu, as well as still larger creatures such as giraffe. Once a kill was made the animal would be butchered and some meat would be cooked and eaten while the remainder would be dried in the sun as 'biltong'. This easy method of preservation produces a chewy but tasty snack that will last many weeks. Unlike their predecessors, kills on these hunting trips were made with guns. These often antiquated weapons had arrived in the area through trade with early white hunters, when the tracking skills of the Bushmen were greatly appreciated. Several groups of Bushmen had used these new weapons to hunt elephant, contributing greatly both to the ivory trade and to the decimation of these huge animals. As the Bangwato gained influence and control of the area, many guns were confiscated and those Tyua who wanted to keep theirs knew to hide them well. Twai Twai was the proud owner of an ancient muzzle-loading rifle, that, while perhaps long past use in conflict, was still a very effective weapon against game.

After falling out with Rekisang's mother, by 1943 Twai Twai was living with his latest wife, Dambe, in the small village of Nata on the edge of the salt pans. Nata lay on the main road, if a dirt track deserved such a name, to the north. This was known as the Hunters Road and led to Kasane and the Zambian border, nearly 300 miles away. Just to the north of the village a branch of the road led west to the town of Maun at the mouth of the Okavango Delta. Just as today, Nata provided a rest stop for travellers. In addition, it was home to a Witwatersrand Native Labour Association (WNLA) camp. WNLA provided work in the South African gold mines and Nata's position on the junction of two of the main tracks made it an ideal recruitment centre, as well as providing a break for labour hired in Zambia on their 800-mile journey south.

As the coldest of the Kalahari winter nights passed, Twai Twai, now widely recognised as the local headman, once again set about organising a hunting trip. This would be made with his friend Tammai, who, though light-skinned and nowhere near as imposing physically as Twai Twai, owned a gun, and Keree, another large dark-skinned Tyua. They would take some of their children, both male and female, and make a camp out in the bush. From here the men would range on their sole horse and two donkeys to hunt.

RHODESIA, 1943

For the second time in his career Gordon was welcomed by the bright lights of Durban. Even though he had seen them before, on his journey to Egypt, they still held a fascination for him. Not only did Durban seem like a very exotic location for a boy from a Welsh mining village, but the war seemed a long way away and life in the port appeared to have been untouched by the conflict. It was hard to compare the hardships he had experienced in Russia with the thriving happy city in front of him.

He had made some good friends on the sail down the east coast of Africa, many of them also prospective pilots bound for one of the many flying training schools that had mushroomed across southern Africa. After a very short stay at Clairewood Camp in Durban, Gordon was shepherded aboard a train that over the next two days made its way to Bulawayo. For those new to Africa this was a fascinating experience, partly due to the scenery and partly to the number of black faces – something new to many of the passengers. From the coast at Durban, the steam engine puffed its way upward through the Drakensburg Mountains and onwards to the goldfields of Johannesburg. From there it was a short trip to Mafeking and then it was a full day's trip through the Bechuanaland Protectorate. For those still awake, the view from the windows made it clear that civilisation, as they knew it, was getting farther and farther away. Durban, Johannesburg and, to some extent, Mafeking had clearly been European settlements, but Bechuanaland was real Africa. Towns on the route might have one or two 'real' buildings, but the rest were just a sea of mud huts. And the towns were far apart, with hours of literally nothing but stunted acacia bush in between. Eventually, Gordon and his new friends, Harry Tait and Walter Adamson, chugged to a halt at Plumtree on the Southern

Rhodesia border. They must have wondered how and why pilots from not only all over Britain, but from all over the Empire, were being sent to what seemed like the end of the world to be trained.

The reasons could be traced back to the outbreak of war when the entire embryonic Southern Rhodesian Air Force (SRAF), comprising nine antiquated biplanes, had decamped for Kenya and the border with Italian Somaliland. 'A' and 'B' Flights were merged to form No. 1 Squadron SRAF. Back in Rhodesia, Bulawayo and Salisbury flying clubs were raided for instructors and aeroplanes for a new training school at Hillside, on the outskirts of the capital. Initially this was unable to cope with the demand and pilots were sent to Habbaniyah, near Baghdad, and later to become famous for its siege, to complete their advanced flying training.

The first half of 1940 saw sixty-two pilots gain their wings and a further fifteen complete their advanced training, a remarkable achievement given the availability of only six instructors and twelve assorted biplanes commandeered from the flying clubs. From this small beginning the Rhodesian Air Training Group would develop.

As early as October 1939, the Southern Rhodesian government had suggested that the country could supply and maintain three squadrons for the RAF. This would include all the necessary training. However, this proposal was dwarfed by what the British Government suggested. Recognising that the need for trained pilots was going to grow exponentially, Britain requested the creation of three pairs of flying schools, one pair at Salisbury, one pair at Bulawayo and the final pair at Gwelo. The selection of these sites followed surveys looking for areas with sufficient water and with a low risk of malaria, both important factors for incoming trainees fresh from Britain and encountering Africa for the first time. Despite the care taken, insufficient rainfall often led to water restrictions with RAF Moffat, Gwelo, being the worst affected. At least one Englishman got into hot water, literally and metaphorically, for having a bath rather than the proscribed twice-weekly showers.

By February 1940 a Group Headquarters had taken residence in Jameson Avenue, and nearby Cranbourne had taken delivery of its first Oxfords and Harvards. These aircraft were assembled and flown up from Durban, as the packing crates they were shipped in were too large for the local railways. The following month saw the first arrival of RAF personnel, under Squadron Leader Eady, consisting of eleven officers and ninety-two other ranks, and these saw the incorporation of the Rhodesian Air Training Group (RATG) into the rapidly growing Empire Air Training Scheme (EATS). This in turn was part of the British Commonwealth Air Training Plan, an agreement signed between Great Britain and its dominions, Canada, Australia and New Zealand. As a colony, rather than a self-governing dominion, Rhodesia was not part of these negotiations and was the last country to officially join the EATS, but was the first to turn out qualified pilots. It is perhaps little known that a similar scheme had operated in Canada during the First World War. More than 3,000 pilots for the Royal Flying Corps, and from April 1918 the Royal Air Force, gained their wings in American-supplied Curtiss Jennys above the wide open spaces of the Canadian countryside.

Under the direction of Group Captain Steele, the Rhodesian branch of EATS grew dramatically over the next two years, with four bases around Salisbury, three in the Gwelo area, and four in and around Bulwayo. Each region had an Elementary Flying Training School (EFTS) for basic flight training, a Service Flying Training School (SFTS) that taught navigation and basic military aviation skills, such as gunnery and bombing, and a Maintenance Unit (MU). Most of the bases were built from scratch, with everything from the front gate to the officer's mess, from the headquarter offices to the fire tender station, going up in record time. Bungalows were built for officers and married airmen, complete with a single room building in the garden, something that might have puzzled those who had not been to white-run southern Africa before. These one-room apartments were for the black servants. Another feature of all the bases was the excellent provision for sports. As well as football and rugby fields, most bases had excellent outdoor swimming pools too.

While the countryside and accommodation may have differed, similar arrangements were also in place in Australia, Canada, New Zealand, South Africa, the United States and, for the lucky ones, the West Indies. Generally, the sites chosen offered good flying weather and were a long way away from any enemy air activity.

Training was often eventful and not always smooth – this Southern Rhodesian Air Force Tiger Moth came to a sticky end. (*Master Tech. Joe Bugler*)

Gordon arrived in Bulawayo on 9 December 1942 and was immediately bussed, or more accurately 'lorried', to Hillside Camp. This was one of the few bases that was not new. It was a converted army barracks, but despite this the accommodation was comfortable and the sports facilities excellent.

Gordon had met Walter Adamson on the boat to Durban and by the time they arrived at Hillside they were already good friends. Walter was a couple of years older than Gordon and had celebrated his twenty-third birthday during the journey from Egypt. Like many his age, he had volunteered as soon as the war started, but bureaucracy had delayed his call up until the end of 1939. Like Gordon, he had hoped to become a pilot and he was posted to 2 Flying Training School, but before he could start the course he was sent to Egypt where he had spent the next two years. Shorter than Gordon, Walter made up for his lack of height with his Yorkshire bluffness and his pride in his Castleford roots. Another new friendship was that formed with the Scot Harry Tait. Harry had also joined up early in the war, leaving his native Edinburgh to protect the naval base at Scapa Flow as a radar operator. Given this experience, when Harry's application for aircrew training was accepted he fully expected to be trained as a navigator rather than a pilot.

While many of Gordon's group had similar stories to tell, having been accepted onto aircrew training after a couple of years in other trades, there were also plenty of raw recruits among them. It could not have been easy for those with service experience to arrive at Hillside, as every member of the course was treated as if they had just joined up. A welcome speech by the CO was followed by medical inspections and allocation of quarters. After briefly settling in, the new arrivals were subject to endless square-bashing and drill. Parades and inspections did not amuse those that had already seen active service. However, training lectures and cockpit instruction gave some realisation of how close they were to learning to fly properly. This provided enough encouragement to ensure that the three friends went on to pass their exams and move onto the next part of the course.

MISSING

2

RAF INDUNA

RAF Induna had gained its name from a flat-topped hill a few miles to the north-east of Bulawayo, N'Thabas-Induna, translating as 'Hill of the Headman'. This suggests it had once been part of Great Zimbabwe, where the rulers of a town would live on top of such a place. The job of this station, as an elementary flying school, was to take would-be pilots and turn them into efficient fliers in the least amount of time.

Tiger Moths were used for this basic training. These classic de Havilland aeroplanes had seen countless airmen take their first flights, but the local environment did put them under extra strain. For a start, Induna was situated at 4,000 feet above sea level, or roughly halfway to the Moth's ceiling in hot conditions. And the conditions were hot – temperatures of over 100°F were common. The tropical sun would heat the earth, causing severe turbulence that often ruled out flying during the hottest parts of the day. This meant

Thousands of pilots took their first flights in the trusty Tiger Moth. (*Botswana Aviation Art*)

that flying usually started at 6 a.m., with inexperienced pilots back on the ground by 9 a.m. It was considered that those with more flying hours could cope with the bumpier air until about midday. If necessary, some flying was also done after teatime once the turbulence started to subside.

Other than the limitations imposed by local conditions, the training syllabus was that being taught in flying schools throughout the Empire. This was laid out in Air Publication 1732, the 'Instructors' Handbook of Elementary Flying Training'. This rather thick pamphlet set out twenty-eight exercises, starting with cockpit familiarity and ending with formation flying, that prospective pilots were expected to master. These exercises could be combined; for example, exercises 7 and 8, climbing and descending, could be taught, or practised, in the same flight.

Gordon, Walter and Harry were all posted to the same course and would have undergone several hours of ground school together before their instructors gave them their first air experience flight (exercise 3, following on from cockpit familiarity and preparation for flight). This was the same for the other seventy-seven men on the programme.

Life for the budding pilots at this time was fun. They all had been promoted to flight sergeants and, although for most this was an 'acting' rank, the extra income was appreciated. Bulawayo was relatively close by and had an exciting night life, including the infamous Bodega Bar. Regular 'bush bashing' trips were organised, especially to the nearby Matobo Game Reserve. This region of unusual rock formations was a particular favourite, being strikingly beautiful as a well as having a range of large game. The Matopos consisted of more than 150 square miles of granite kopjes weathered into the strangest shapes, with boulders of enormous sizes balanced precariously on top of one another. For those in need of exercise, a trip to Cecil Rhodes' grave atop a bald smooth hill aptly named 'World's View' was in order. He and the other pilots would have had a chance to feed the rainbow skinks that inhabit the cracks between the stones.

The brightly coloured lizards had become used to visitors to the grave and, even today, will come when called in the hope of a treat. Bushman rock art, dating back at least 2,000 years, and an interesting series of caves formed another distraction. Most pilots also had the opportunity to travel further afield, with Victoria Falls being a popular destination. There were regular sports meetings against the other RAF stations and each area produced its own service magazine. Perhaps best of all, there was unlimited food. For those who had been used to service rations the idea of fresh fruit on demand was amazing, but nothing compared to being able to help themselves to as many helpings of bacon and eggs as they could manage.

The only people that were not happy were some of those teaching the cadet pilots. Before fully fledged pilots were posted out of the Rhodesian Air Training Group, the cream of each course was sent to RAF Norton, near Salisbury. At this elite station they would learn to become instructors and be retained in the RATG to train more students. RAF Norton had a certain refined, academic air about it and it could have been considered something of a flying

The tame and ever-hungry rainbow skinks that live around Cecil Rhodes' grave atop the Matopo Hills. (*Botswana Aviation Art*)

university. As can be imagined, those retained had a range of reactions to being held back as their friends and comrades were posted to front-line squadrons closer to home. Some were relieved, some were stoical, some disappointed and some little less than furious. Two instructors who were kept in Rhodesia against their will came up with the bright idea of giving their superiors no choice but to post them on. This scheme involved a mock bombing attack on Bulawayo city centre. When the big day came, they put on a display that the Rhodesian city has never since seen the like of. Low pass after low pass, up and down the wide streets of Bulawayo they roared, often below the level of the buildings to each side of their wing tips. Their self-imposed mission was a partial success. The two pilots were relieved of their instructor jobs and were posted. Unfortunately for them, their new post was still in Rhodesia and they were still involved in training. They were both given the job of piloting target tugs, flying up and down trailing a large banner behind them while ham-fisted new pilots practised their shooting!

Despite the carefully chosen sites, Gordon and his comrades arrived at the start of the malaria season. A shortage of quinine had led to a spike in cases the previous year, but a combination of new supplies and stockpiling through the safe months of June, August and September meant that by the end of 1943 all the airmen were being administered the prophylactic. In addition, mosquito nets were in mandatory use. Tuberculosis and typhoid had been particular concerns of the air force authorities, but inoculations had meant that not a single case of either had been reported in the six months before Gordon's arrival. Flu was the greatest threat at that time of year for those in Bulawayo. Another hazard for the hard-living airmen far from home were the ever-present venereal diseases, with just under 200 cases being diagnosed in 1942. Given that the forces population at this time was 10,000, this was considered not too bad. However, medical officers on every station gave regular lectures on how to avoid VD by taking 'proper precautions'.

In fact, the chance of catching an embarrassing disease was similar to that of being killed during training. The April–June report into the health of the Southern Rhodesian training scheme listed twenty-six flying deaths, compared with twenty-eight cases of VD. Of these accidents, twelve fatalities were in the Bulawayo region. There were also two fatal road accidents during that period. This report concluded that the overall health of the groups continued to be good. Some evidence for this can be taken from the surviving baptism records from the Gwelo section. Here, there were seventeen babies born between July 1942 and June 1943. All of these were to married couples at Guinea Fowl, Thornhill or Moffat. Guinea Fowl was the most remote of any of the RAF stations, being more than eleven miles out of town. Its inhabitants considered it, with some justification, to be well and truly the back of beyond. It should not have come as any surprise then that the reproduction rate there was double that of the other two stations!

Gordon's logbook would have rapidly filled with dual control hours, as his instructors showed him the basics of flight. It would also have started to gain a number of certifications, confirming that he understood the aircraft's systems and that he knew how to swing a propeller and safely start the Tiger Moth. After between eight and fifteen hours of instruction he would have been given the opportunity of his first solo flight, something that no pilot ever forgets. This was far from the initial training over, however. At least fifteen hours were required in the station's Link Trainer, a very early form of flight simulator. This bellows-powered blue box gave pilots a chance to practise instrument flying without leaving the ground. Once this was mastered then another five hours in a covered Moth cockpit were added. At the same time, more intensive flying manoeuvres and aerobatics were included, initially with an instructor and then solo. Often flying twice a day, the flying hours soon started to add up.

Navigation also formed a part of the course, teaching basic map-reading along with formation flying. This was one of the last skills taught, by which time a fair proportion of the eighty men who had started the course would have been 'scrubbed out'. Failing the course, they would have been posted to other flying duty courses and continued as gunners, flight engineers or navigators. This was the fate of just under 40 per cent of those who began pilot training.

Part of the required reading for the budding pilots was *Tee Emm*, an Air Ministry publication that was intended as a serious instructional read, yet one that was heavily dressed up in humour. To accomplish this difficult task the Air Ministry relied upon the writing talents available at *Punch*, particularly those of Anthony Armstrong Willis and William Hooper. It introduced a generation of fliers to the bumbling antics of Pilot Officer Prune who offered such gems of advice as 'If we just steer west we will get home' and 'I never make a test burst as we have to clean our own guns'. Bill Hooper's creation was much loved, although at one point he had to write to *Tee Emm*'s letter section in an attempt to prove that he was real. In one memorable feature-length episode in *Punch*, Prune and his colleagues spend a valuable night in the mess discussing how flies land on the ceiling. A tricky aerodynamic problem, if ever there was one.

Tee Emm was short for 'Technical Manual' and it did include much sensible advice on air safety, written by experts. Much of this guidance focused on navigation of a higher standard than Prune's. The need for good pre-flight preparation of maps and a mental rehearsal of landmarks the pilot would see on the flight was emphasised, as were the more technical points of using a compass. In 1942 the publication started awarding its own decoration to aircrew. In true *Punch* style, the Most Highly Derogatory Order of the Irremovable Finger (MHDOIF) was in a very different class to the VC and, although its recipients had their names redacted in the magazine, no doubt many were still embarrassingly recognised. An early award of the MHDOIF was made to a bomber crew whose navigator had set up his compass incorrectly over Germany and had been flying a reciprocal course. Realising his mistake, the aircraft, now short of fuel, turned around with the pilot doubting they could reach England. When the fuel eventually ran out, the pilot made a good forced landing and, once his crew had safely disembarked, set fire to his aeroplane to save it from falling into enemy hands. Setting off across the fields to make good their escape, the unlucky airmen soon came across the Rose and Crown, a pub well known to them all.

Two of the most challenging drills on the syllabus were numbers 21 and 22: precautionary and forced landings. As the instructor's handbook pointed out, forced landings were rare and usually due to engine failure. The reason for engine failure was, nine times out of ten, running out of fuel, a lesson drilled into the hearts of all new pilots. The secret to a good forced landing was ensuring that the pilot had sufficient height when the emergency occurred. The special case was the event of engine failure on takeoff, where the only advice was to land straight ahead, avoiding obstacles as much as possible. These forced landing exercises would have started at Induna, with the instructor showing how a stationary propeller would affect the gliding angle. Following this, cadets would be constantly asked to pick out fields suitable for emergencies. This was not easy given the Rhodesian landscape, which consisted mainly of low scrub, with few open spaces. The occasional road or farm gave some choice, as would a dried-up riverbed in a real emergency. Once pilots had experience in picking fields, the instructor would then simulate an engine failure and the pupil had to make a 'deadstick' landing. According to the handbook, the aim of the exercise was to make such actions second nature so that a pilot would not waste time wondering what to do in a real emergency.

After ninety hours of flying, half of which was solo, Gordon's logbook gained another big stamp. This summed up his flying time to date, including five hours of night-flying, along with a rating as 'above average' as a pilot and 'average' as a pilot navigator. 'Nil' was the comment for the 'faults that need watching' box. This was then signed off by the Chief Flying Instructor and the Wing Commander in charge of Induna. The date was 25 June 1943.

RAF KUMALO

After a few days celebratory leave, Gordon and his good friends were posted to 21 Service Flying Training School (SFTS) at Kumalo, right on the edge of Bulawayo. Despite having more than twice the flying hours required for a private pilot's licence today, they still had not been awarded their 'wings'. This would come at the end of the course, where their basic skills would be turned into something the Air Force could use.

In fact, the syllabus at 21 SFTS was split into two parts. The first part was a conversion course to the twin-engine Airspeed Oxford. The Oxford has been forgotten by many today, but few aircraft could have done as much to help win the war. It was a development of the Envoy, infamous in southern Africa for the crash that had killed several members of the RAF boxing team, the one Al Deere had been lucky to avoid. The aircraft involved in that incident was one of seven 'Convertible Envoys'. These could be fitted with bomb racks and a gun turret on top of the fuselage. The South African order to some degree paved the way for the Oxford, as it showed the flexibility of the design. Airspeed had been founded in 1931 by Alfred Hessel Tiltman and Neville Shute Norway, both of whom were better known with one name less. Tiltman, who was responsible for the design of the Oxford, usually omitted Alfred and was better known as Hessel. Norway, who left the company just before the war, was better known as the author Neville Shute. Under this name he gained considerable fame and many of his books were later filmed, such as *A Town Like Alice*. The Airspeed Company had been taken over by de Havilland in 1940, the more mature aircraft manufacturers taking control from Swan Hunters.

The twin-engine Airspeed AS.10 Oxford was used for training in navigation, bombing and gunnery, and radio operation. (Author's collection)

The aircraft itself was a thoroughly modern design, being a semi-monocoque cantilever monoplane with retractable landing gear. Perhaps the most groundbreaking part of the design was that it was intended from the start to be a full crew trainer, capable of instructing pilots, flight engineers, wireless operators, bomb aimers, navigators and gunners. To allow for this, the second pilot's seat could be removed, giving space for a bomb aimer to lie and aim through the clear nose. Alternatively, this seat could be pushed back, allowing the occupant to use the navigator's plotting table. A wireless station was included in the cabin and, on almost all early aircraft, a gun turret at the rear of the cabin completed the set-up. Over 8,000 of these versatile aircraft were built, and it is estimated that at least a quarter of all RAF pilots during the war trained on them. Half of them were assembled at Airspeed's Portsmouth plant, while the rest were built at the company's shadow plant in Dorset, or by de Havilland, Percival or Standard Motors, at Hatfield, Luton and Coventry, respectively. The Oxford moniker came from the RAF's tradition of giving names with educational connotations to its training aircraft.

The three young men from Britain must have made their way to Kumalo with a tinge of regret. Some of their comrades from Induna had been posted to Harvard flight schools. This big single-engine trainer was the next step on the way to becoming a fighter pilot. The posting to an Oxford school suggested a life of multi-engine 'bus driving'. However, this was not guaranteed, as once converted to their new aircraft all the trainee pilots followed an identical syllabus.

The Harvard schools had had their share of interesting, and sometimes tragic, incidents. One pilot had a very lucky escape when he got totally lost during a night-flying exercise and found himself running out of fuel more than 500 miles from home. He bailed out over the edge of the Kalahari, way over the Bechuanaland border, and broke his leg upon landing. Having crawled under a thorn bush, he was subsequently rescued by a young cattle herder near the village of Moiyabana. He was then taken the 30 miles north to the hospital in Serowe, before being returned to Rhodesia. During the search for the missing pilot, the runway of the landing strip at Serowe was extended by the order of Tshekedi Khama so that the Harvards of the search party could safely operate from it.

Those destined for fighters would have been posted to a Harvard flight school.

While that story ended happily, some incidents had more grue-some outcomes, and not just for the pilots. All Service Flying Training Schools included bombing on their syllabuses and this would often take place over dams or other easily recognisable areas. There were six ranges in all and the limits of each one were set out in the 'Flying Regulations for RATG [Rhodesian Air Training Group]'. One par-ticular range was set up with a buoy as the target on a large reservoir, approached from the river end and exiting over the dam. Judging height over still water is very difficult at the best of times and near misses must have been common. Today there is a Harvard display team in South Africa whose party piece is to make a low pass over water with their wheels touching the surface, kicking up an impressive amount of spray, but there is a big difference between pilots with tens of thousands of flying hours and trainees with less than 200. These low-flying aircraft must have been a magnet for young boys of all races and this might explain why one young African boy was on the dam when a Harvard made a misjudged pass. The pilot was obviously too low and was probably so concentrated on getting himself out of mis-chief that he did not even see the small figure on the rampart. The boy was killed instantly and this incident caused some problems with the local people, with some believing the child had been 'murdered'.

Gordon would have been well aware of the low-flying regulations. Flying below 1,000 feet was prohibited at all times. If a pilot found himself under this level he was expected to make an entry in the 'Low-Flying Book', meaning a trip to the Chief Flying Instructor's office, where it was kept. Other restrictions were a 2,000-feet minimum height over built-up areas and game reserves, including the local Matopos. This meant having no opportunity to buzz your friends on their bush treks. Victoria Falls was unusually well pro-tected, with a 75-mile exclusion zone that could only be entered with express permission from RATG headquarters.

RAF Kumalo was right on the edge of the city centre, being only a mile or so down the road from Harare. A left turn off the main road would take you immediately into the administration area with its many single-storey buildings and offices. Behind these, and hidden from the main road by the long grass, stubby trees and a slight dip, was the main concrete runway, surrounded by a large grassy area. Just beyond the opposite ends of the runway were a sewage works and a cemetery. With characteristic black humour it was often pointed out that new pilots would eventually end up deep in one of these. To the northern edge of the aerodrome, the Harare railway line curved past the boundary fence. About 5,000 people were working at Kumalo at any one time and the base provided three churches and a cinema with a different film every night of the week to meet their needs. Best of all in many airmen's eyes were the number of attractive WAAFs, with the Polish girls being favourite in many a smitten young man's eye. The base was also home to a large number of native Askaris. Unlike their Batswana neighbours, Rhodesian politics meant that black troops were used exclusively for second-line duties. For the Ndebele descendants of Mzilikazi's great warriors, it must have been extremely frustrating to have been treated as second-class citizens, with only a relative handful trusted with rifles for base guard duty. Segregation, while not strictly legal, was enforced. Indeed, a visit to Bulawayo could be made easily without having to communicate with a single black face. Townships had grown up around the city, deprived areas where few whites would ever venture. For those who had already served with black troops, and even aircrew, this was something of an eye-opener. However, most pilots seem to have accepted it as being normal, a reflection of pre-war attitudes to race.

As at Induna, the course at Kumalo consisted of numbered exercises. Gordon's first flight in an Oxford would have probably included drills 1 to 8 – Air Experience and Familiarity, Effect of Controls, Taxiing, Straight and Level Flying, Climbing and Gliding, Medium Turns, Taking Off into Wind, and Final Approach and Landing. If new pilots were lucky, instructors might give a demonstration of low-flying as well. The biggest difference from Induna was the fact that pupils tended to be assigned to a single instructor. Gordon and Walter maintained their close partnership, both being assigned to Alfred 'Alf' Eves.

After about nine flights, the trainees were given their first solo in the Oxford, gaining an extra certificate in their logbook stating that they understood the fuel and oil systems of the training aircraft. Soon afterwards, formation flying and low-flying would be started, at first with the instructor present. Roughly half of Gordon's flights would now be solo ones, with navigation, instrument and night-flying becoming more important. The next crucial step occurred after about eighty hours on the Oxford, with the cadet pilots being certified not only to fly the Oxford, but also to carry passengers and act as safety pilots for other trainees. From now on Gordon would mainly fly with his classmates, rather than with an instructor. It would have been a natural choice for Gordon to pair up with his friend from Yorkshire, Walter Adamson. The pair flew their first sortie, a photographic flight, in the middle of August.

Walter and Gordon took turns as captain as the flying became more varied and interesting. Formation flying with the other pupils, instrument flying and navigation sorties became progressively more challenging. At the same time more warlike missions were added, forcing the pair to act as a team. Bombing sorties to one of the six ranges, both at high- and low-level, added to the sense that the train-ees were getting closer to the day when they would see action for real. This was especially true when formation strikes were practised.

Airspeed Oxford 'office'. (*Toby Williams*)

Photography and reconnaissance missions added to the skill set, while simulated artillery spotting gave the pilots a reminder that the Air Force did not act alone.

One exercise highlighted by the mythical Pilot Officer Prune in *Tee Emm* would not have been practised, however. The only Oxford aircrew to be awarded the magazine's MHDOIF award was a flight sergeant who was a passenger on a cross-country exercise. Feeling the need to relieve himself, he opened the Oxford's cabin door in order to carry out the act. The next time the pilot saw him was when he returned to his station with a loosely bundled parachute under his arm.

During this period all the sergeant pilots were given their commission interview. Sadly, there were still many RAF officers who were just as conscious of class as ability. One commanding officer's interview allegedly consisted of only three questions. He believed

The last existing photo of Gordon Edwards. (*Edwards family*)

that a cadet's future could be predicted on their father's profession, whether they had attended a grammar school and their preference for rugby over football.

Alf Eves still gave instruction to Walter and Gordon, especially on navigation and night-flying. Perhaps, the most difficult exercise at this point was the night ground-controlled approach, with Gordon learning to land on moonless nights, trusting to his instruments and the controllers on the ground. Gordon would fly with Alf on about one in six sorties, picking up valuable hints and tips. By this time the prospective pilots had more than 200 flying hours under their belts. This was a remarkable improvement on the desperate days of the Battle of Britain, and an unthinkable number from the days of Biggles. In the Great War it was not unknown for pilots to have less than twenty hours of instruction before being posted to the Western Front. It must also be remembered that most of the pilots on Gordon's course would next be posted not to the front line, but to an Operational Training Unit where their war-flying skills would be honed still further.

Alf would have still been responsible for measuring the progress of his students. This was done through a series of tests, including the Observers test and the Pilot Navigation test. Gordon, Walter and Harry passed these and were well on their way to their wings.

FINAL FLIGHT

At the start of October 1943, Gordon and Walter were well aware that they only had three weeks of their course left. A lot of discussion had gone on between the two as to where they would be posted to next. Given the fact they had been on a twin-engine course, Bomber Command loomed large in these talks although Coastal Command or even Transport Command were possibilities.

By October 1943, Bomber Command was getting well into its stride, largely re-equipped with the four-engine Lancasters and Halifaxes under the command of Arthur Harris, who had come a long way from his Rhodesian bugler-boy days. While lacking some of the glamour of the fighter boys, Bomber Command had had a good year so far. The heroics of 617 Squadron's 'Dam Busters' had generated great publicity and had made heroes of the 'Bomber Boys', for perhaps the first time. Along with the introduction of the new 'heavies', great leaps had been made in the development of technology. H2S, a ground-mapping radar allowing independent navigation, and 'Window', metallic strips cut to the wavelength of German radars that effectively blinded them, had both been introduced. Both these devices had played their part in the destruction of Hamburg, creating a firestorm that had killed more than 30,000 in July.

Coastal Command was another posting they had to consider, although neither fancied the idea of long patrols over the Atlantic in a Sunderland flying boat. They both would have recognised how important the RAF was in the war against the U-boats, but they would have also known that the average Sunderland crew spent more than 200 hours in the air before spotting one of the elusive German submarines. Alternatively, they could have been sent to an anti-shipping squadron where rockets were just becoming the favoured weapon, taking over from the air-dropped torpedo. This would have satisfied the need for excitement the trainee pilots had, but these squadrons had some of the highest loss rates in the entire Air Force.

Neither Gordon nor Walter were interested in being a 'bus driver' with Transport Command. While recognising their vital logistical role, it was hardly the stuff to get the blood of young men racing. Perhaps Gordon's biggest fear was a return to the Middle Eastern theatre, especially now that Italy had been invaded the action was moving back to northern Europe. The fact that the majority of pilots trained in Rhodesia in the first couple of years of the RATG had been sent to the Middle East would have weighed on his mind.

These were the issues on the minds of Edwards and Adamson as they strolled out to their waiting Airspeed Oxford on a sunny Monday morning, the activities of a 'pay day' weekend already fading in their memories. Gordon was captain for this flight and Walter was merely present as an observer, an arrangement they were used to. Having flown together many times since their arrival at Kumalo, taking turns as pilot, they had a good understanding of how each other thought in the air, which had helped cement their friendship.

The mission for the day was a simple navigation exercise: taking off from Kumalo they were to head north-east to Selukwe, turning south-west to Gwanda, before finally turning north back to Kumalo. Take-off was set for 10:45 and both pilots were hoping to be back in time for a slightly late lunch.

Having already signed for the aircraft, they arrived at Airspeed Oxford HN607, a Portsmouth-built turret-equipped version of the versatile trainer. Gordon did the external pre-flight checks with Walter casting a careful eye over his preparations. Starting at the entrance door on the left of the fuselage, Gordon worked his way around the aeroplane in a clockwise fashion, using his checklist as a guide. The left wing would have been checked first, looking for any damage to the surface and that the fuel tank cover was secure. The flap and aileron were followed by the engine, checking for any

Boarding for a navigation sortie with a camera to prove their success.
(*RAF Museum Collection – 1988/0416/S*)

leaks and the condition of the propeller. The port undercarriage was checked next, ensuring that the shock absorber and tyre were fine. The nose, where the external fire extinguishers were kept, was followed by a repeat of the checks so far – this time on the starboard side. Finally, the fuselage panels and the empennage, including both elevators and the rudder, were checked.

Satisfied with the external condition of the aircraft, both pilots climbed aboard to complete the final checks. After ensuring that there were no loose items in the cabin, Gordon checked that the first-aid kit was in place, the fire extinguishers were in position, the crash axe was correctly stowed, and that the engine covers were present and correctly packed away. Finally, before strapping in, he would have checked the presence of the water container. This was not part of the standard Oxford pilot's checklist but had been added locally.

Gordon would have probably reduced the height of his pilot's seat, while Walter would have raised his. This would have been important for the shorter man, as only the pilot's seat could be adjusted in flight. Having sat down, they would have checked the electrical switches, undercarriage setting and that the aircraft was fuelled correctly. The ground crew then would have primed the engines before they were started. In the October warmth this would have been a straightforward procedure.

While the engines warmed up, final checks and preparations would have been made, with the engine starting handle being passed in to the aircraft and stowed, while the flap operations were tested. The direction indicator would have been set according to the compass and, finally, a radio check made. Once the chocks were removed the Oxford would have rumbled gently towards the concrete runway as Gordon checked the compass, artificial horizon and the brakes.

Lined up in a north-westerly direction, once permission for take-off had been granted, the aeroplane's throttle would have been opened slowly, as the Oxford had a tendency to swing to the right and careful engine management was needed to avoid this. As 65 miles per hour was reached, Gordon would have eased the control column back and the large trainer would have taken to the air. The outskirts of Bulawayo and then the city centre must have come into view out of the port window before a gentle turn to the right slid them out of sight again. Height was slowly gained in the warm, thin air and, with a final radio message to Kumalo, the two pilots were on their own.

Levelling out on a course of 080°, the two pilots would have settled down for the 90-mile trip to their first waypoint at Selukwe. Accurate instrument flying was vital, as the bush underneath stretched to the horizon and it offered few distinct features to aid navigation. Obviously, that was the point of these navigation training sorties.

Although small, Selukwe, now known as Shurugwi, did have a couple of features to help the two pilots identify it. First, there was a large, bare granite hill that had given the village its name, and, second, as a gold-mining town it had been connected to Gwelo (now Gweru) by rail. As it was the end of the line, this would have given confidence to Gordon and Walter as they waited for it to drift into view out of the endless scrub.

As the mining centre came into sight, Walter would have made himself busy with the handheld camera. The aim of this was two-fold: to give crews experience of reconnaissance as well as giving instructors a way of checking on their pupils' navigational accuracy. Flying at 125mph, the Oxford was a stable platform for photography, needing little input from the pilot. Although the Oxford had a never-exceed speed of 270mph, this could only be achieved in a dive and 120–130mph gave the best fuel economy. Faster than this, the aircraft gradually lost some of its stability, especially in the fore–aft axis.

With the mining town safely captured on film, Gordon then turned 150° starboard, almost doubling back on his original course. This time the objective was Gwanda, another town owing its name to a nearby hill. Gwanda was the administrative capital of Southern Matabeleland, but, even so, it was home only to a couple of thousand people. Again the fact that a railway ran through the town, this time the Bulawayo–Beitbridge line to South Africa, would have given a good aiming point for the airmen.

Finding the small town, Walter again took a photograph from 7,000 feet before Gordon made his final turn that should have seen the two airmen back at RAF Kumalo within forty minutes.

They were never seen again.

SEARCH

OVERDUE

The flight should have taken about two-and-a-half hours to complete and the aircraft had a good fuel reserve, so there would have been little initial apprehension at RAF Kumalo because of the late arrival of Gordon and Walter.

However, when the Oxford had not returned by the late afternoon, the station commander would have been informed. With no reports of a crash coming in, though given the sparseness of the bush population this was not a great reassurance, the first step would have been to phone the other RATG airfields around Bulawayo to see if the missing pilots had called in there. This would not have been too surprising, a social call or perhaps mechanical problems might have led to a landing at any of the airfields in the area. However, calls to Induna, Hillside and Heany soon confirmed that the two pilots had not been seen. It would have been late afternoon by the time these calls had been made, and the early tropical sunset meant there was only time for a single brief search that evening.

The next day saw a hive of activity at all of the local bases as a full-scale air-search was organised. Initially this comprised loose formations of three aircraft retracing the route taken by Adamson and Edwards the previous day. When this produced no results, sections of three aircraft were then allocated points on the route from which they would conduct 'square searches'. This involved aircraft following the missing aircraft's course so far before turning into the wind and flying straight for four minutes. After a right-angled turn to the left, another four minutes would be flown and another left-hand 90° turn made. This time the legs would last six minutes between the 'corners' of the 'square'. This would be repeated, with the length of each straight being increased every two legs.

This produced a square 'spiral' centred on the original point, providing that allowance for the speed of the current wind was made.

Alf Eves, Gordon and Walter's instructor, was one of many involved in this exercise. His log book shows that he flew five search sorties, each lasting at least three hours, in the days following his pupils' disappearance. These searches went on for more than a week, with no sign of the missing pilots being found. This was especially hard for those who had been part of the same course and who had only a couple of weeks left before they were posted overseas. Friends of the pair, such as Harry Tait, searched in vain and would have a long wait before they found out what had happened to their comrades.

As the mystery deepened the RAF called in the British South African Police (BSAP), the police force for Southern Rhodesia. Their confusing name dated back to their creation as part of the British South African Company, from which they were formed as a mounted paramilitary force. This military association was still in place during the Second World War, with all the force being trained soldiers as well as policemen. Indeed, the BSAP were very proud of their position as the senior regiment of the Rhodesian Army. The war had depleted its manpower for criminal investigations and women had been admitted for the first time in 1941 to take the place of those serving in the front line overseas.

The BSAP posted details to all of its police posts in the eastern half of the country and its horseback officers sought information from villages throughout the region. However, they had no more success than the Air Force in their search. Gordon Edwards and Walter Adamson were, in every sense of the word, 'missing'.

MISSING

OHMS 11.10.1943.

IMMEDIATE FROM AIR MINISTRY KINGSWAY REGRET TO INFORM YOU THAT YOUR SON ACTING SERGEANT GORDON EDWARDS IS REPORTED MISSING AS THE RESULTS OF AIR OPERATIONS 4TH OCTOBER 1944 ENQUIRIES ARE BEING MADE THROUGH VARIOUS ORGANIZATIONS AND ANY FURTHER INFORMATION RECEIVED WILL BE IMMEDIATELY COMMUNICATED TO YOU LETTER CONFIRMING THIS TELEGRAM FOLLOWS.

Air Ministry, London
12 October 1944

Madam,

I am commanded by the Air Council to confirm the telegram in which we were notified that your son, Acting Sergeant Gordon Edwards, Royal Air Force, is missing as the result of air operations on the 4th October 1944.

Your son was flying an Oxford aircraft on a training sortie and has failed to return. This does not necessarily mean that he is killed or wounded. Enquiries will continue to be made through official and local sources. As soon as any definite news is received, you will be at once informed.

The Air Council desire me to express their sincere sympathy with you in your present anxiety.

I am, Madam,
        Your obedient Servant,
                for Air Ministry.

These bald missives were how many thousands of mothers found out that their beloved sons were 'missing', that terrible term that leaves just a trace of hope for those at home. Too often they would be followed within days by the final confirmation of death. In the case of Gordon and Walter the uncertainty would last a lot longer, certainly well into 1944.

Sarah Edwards received the letter described on the day that Italy declared war upon Germany, their former Nazi allies. She kept her news to herself and did not let anybody else know, not even Gordon's father or sister. Perhaps she received a little comfort from a letter from the Officer Commanding RAF Kumalo, that described Gordon's piloting ability as 'well above average' and that he was 'greatly liked and respected by both his instructors and brother pupil pilots'.

Mrs Edwards was devastated by the apparent loss of her only son, and the lack of certainty did not help her state of mind. It might have been that she still had a glimmer of hope, and by not sharing her grief she was protecting her family until there was definite news.

TRIAL

LOBATSI

The plane had gone missing on 4 October 1943, and over the next two months the grisly tale of what had happened to the two pilots slowly emerged. By the 28 January the following year, a preliminary hearing was underway in the Magistrate's Court in Francistown and the bizarre details of the case were making news around the world, even earning a couple of paragraphs in *Time* magazine. However, it was soon clear that the magnitude of the alleged crimes was so great that the case was quickly adjourned in order to be moved to the High Court in Lobatsi.

Lobatsi was the biggest town close to the South African border and was not only on the railway from Mafeking, but was also less than an hour's drive away through the bush. The town had a largish European population, both English and Dutch, but was still little more than a one-street town. This street meandered through the

The High Court in Lobatsi, here seen unchanged in the 1960s. (*Sandy Grant*)

pleasant rolling hills that surrounded the settlement and ended at the abattoir, where cattle were killed before being loaded onto railcars to make the journey down south. Live cattle were also processed in the town, especially as the cold house was now being used by the Army. The courthouse was situated at the opposite end of town and formed part of the administrative enclave. The District Commissioner shared his office with the court, which formed one side of a dusty open courtyard. The jail and police station made up the other two sides.

After further investigation the full trial eventually opened on Monday, 25 September 1944. Being tried for the alleged murder of the airmen were eight Basarwa. This group comprised three men, the alleged ring-leaders, and five women, who were understood to have taken lesser roles in the supposed crime. However, they were all charged with murder and would face the gallows if found guilty. The men involved were Twai Twai Molele, Tammai Mashupatsela and Keree Koetobe, while the five women were named as Bene Whange, Chenda Resetora, Anchere Maroto, Autwa Mashupatsela and Haukwe Whange.

The main officials involved were Justice K.M. de Beer, who was to hear the case in the absence of Walter Huggard, who usually took High Court cases, but was acting as High Commissioner in Pretoria, William Forbes Mackenzie and Vivien Frederick Ellenberger, both District Commissioners in the relevant territories, and Seitshiro Moshweu, who acted as the native assessor. Leading the prosecution was Edwin Ridgill Roper, the Attorney General. The 59-year-old Roper had been born in Queenstown, South Africa, but had worked in the protectorate on and off since 1937. He had served with distinction in the First World War, being awarded the Distinguished Service Order, the Military Cross and the *Croix de Guerre* before joining the bar in Cape Town. He would eventually retire in 1969 as President of the Court of Appeal of the Republic of Botswana. Percy Fraenkel represented the male defendants and Reginald Kelly the females. Fraenkel was an obvious choice for the defence as he was a very well respected lawyer from Mafeking, often representing the government in cases when the Attorney General was absent. Fraenkel was the senior partner at Fraenkel and Gericke, while Kelly was a partner at Minchin and Kelly, the other Mafeking law firm. Kelly had joined up at the start of the Second World War, but had returned from North Africa the previous year after the death of his brother. Two Batswana, by the names of Sebanana and Sedimo, were also to play an integral role in the proceedings, the former translating the defendants' evidence into Setswana and the latter then translating again, this time into English. This strange game of Chinese whispers grew to have an increasing effect on the direction the case would take.

What follows is a day-by-day account of the trial as described in the surviving court documents. The main change is that the evidence of each witness has been brought together as a single narrative before any cross-examination. There are several reasons for taking this approach. First, it allows the evidence to be placed in a logical order as the many questions were asked out of sequence, with the legal teams jumping back and forth between certain points of interest. Second, in many places the evidence being given was hampered by either translation or a lack of suitable Setswana words – leading to much repetition and confusion. Finally, it allows a neat insertion of explanatory notes which, hopefully, will allow the reader a clearer picture of Botswana in the 1940s.

MONDAY 25 SEPTEMBER

With the courthouse packed to such an extent that latecomers had to make do with sitting on the hard dirt and grass outside of the main building, the trial got underway with the calling of the first witness, an instructor pilot from RAF Kumalo. He was sworn in with the usual formalities before he turned to face the Attorney General, who opened the questioning. To his right sat the defendants along a wooden bench, the girls with their arms around one another for support. Smartly dressed in European style, including hats for the men, they cut significantly different figures from the semi-nomadic Bushmen that had set out semi-naked on a hunting party nearly a year earlier.

Witness for the Prosecution – Flight Lieutenant Ronald Payne

I am a member of the RAF stationed at Kumalo near Bulawayo. I knew both pilots that went missing and would describe Edwards as fair-haired and five feet ten tall, Adamson was shorter – about five foot seven – and he was dark-haired.

On the fourth of October 1943, Airspeed Oxford HN607 took off on a navigation training sortie and I hereby produce the flight authorisation book. Edwards was the aircraft captain and Adamson was acting as his observer. The course was Kumalo to Selukwe, Selukwe to Gwanda, Gwanda to Kumalo. The aircraft did not return and I did not see Adamson or Edwards again. When they did not return their kit was put into storage immediately.

The two pilots would have worn Khaki drill, with either shorts or long trousers being allowed. If flying at altitude they might have also worn jackets. Shirts might have carried rank insignia and both pilots were acting sergeants. If they were wearing shorts then their socks would have been khaki, with long trousers they could have been brown or black. If they were carrying money it could have been British, Rhodesian, or South African, as all are in common use in Bulawayo.

Around three weeks after the plane went missing we received a report saying that the plane had been found intact near Nata, in the Bechuanaland Protectorate, and on the fifth of November I accompanied Wing Commander Grace on a flight from Kumalo to the missing aircraft. We inspected the aircraft and found it to be in perfect condition. We refuelled it before flying it back to Kumalo the next day. Despite being in good condition there were several items missing from the Oxford. These included the compass, the Very pistol, the axe, the water container, the observers parachute pack, and the parachute canopy. It was a standing order that parachutes should be carried on all flights, so it would have been very unusual for the missing crew not to have taken theirs. The parachute pack or container is a metal-framed box about two foot by eighteen inches, covered in khaki canvass and secured with elastic bands. The axe is of the same type as the one in the courtroom.

It is interesting to compare Payne's description of Edwards as being dark-haired to the surviving photos of him, and also to note the short and apparently routine description of the recovery flight. This was far from a normal trip and would certainly have been an interesting journey. Contemporary accounts describe Grace and Payne having to fly over the salt pan where the missing Oxford was several times in order to scare away a large group of warthogs. Wildlife in this part of Africa could be a problem at smaller airfields, let alone in the genuine wilderness of the Magkgadikgadi

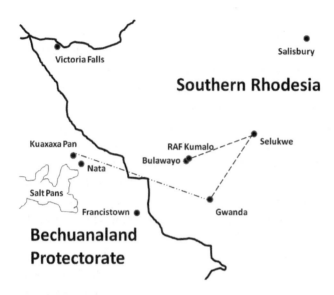

The route of the final flight.

pans. And while hiking into the tame bush around Bulawayo had become a way of filling in time for many RAF crew, that would not have been any real preparation for facing the real thing – something that would have hit home when Grace and Payne came across a lion kill close to the abandoned aircraft.

Flight Lieutenant Payne was then subject to a gentle cross-examination where Fraenkel, the legal representative for the three men, was very interested in the clothing the missing pilots were wearing. Payne described the leather flying helmets worn as standard, and indicated the ear and microphone attachments left in the aircraft suggested that these had been worn by the missing pilots. Pilots might carry other caps with them, but peaked caps were generally only worn for formal occasions – although many pilots felt it gave them a dashing look. The missing pilots would definitely have been wearing socks, he said. The missing Very pistol, used to fire flares, was described as being 10 inches long with a bore of 1½ inches.

Kelly, the defence lawyer for the women charged, then asked for details about the flight that went missing. Payne described the maximum endurance of the Oxford as being five hours, but in this case petrol was only carried for about three and a half to four hours flying, but that this should have been sufficient as the 400-mile exercise should not have taken more than three hours. Payne then explained that the aircraft was understood to have flown the first two legs of the flight without problems as they had taken a photo of the last checkpoint at Gwanda. If they had not turned at Gwanda they would have flown into Bechuanaland, but at a point much further south than where they were found. The aircraft was found about 250 miles from Kumalo and the area where it landed was one that Payne would have chosen himself in such an emergency. Kuaxaxa pan was a wide expense of salty dried white earth, surrounded by the customary scrub. It would have provided a perfect surface for an aircraft to land on while it was dry.

Prosecution witness – Wing Commander Eric Basil Grace

Wing Commander Grace had been the Officer Commanding RAF Kumalo at the time of Adamson's and Edwards' disappearance, but by the time the trial had started, he had been posted to the Middle East. The court allowed, with the permission of the defence, his short written testimony at the pre-trial hearing in Francistown to be submitted in full:

On the 5th of November 1943 I received instructions to recover a missing Airspeed Oxford. I left later the same day and landed next to HN607. There was nobody with the aircraft although the compass, the Very pistol, the axe, the water container, the observers parachute pack and the parachute canopy were all missing.

I flew the aircraft back to Kumalo the following day where Leading Aircraftsman Walton was responsible for its overhaul. I do not know what happened to the missing pilots.

Prosecution Witness – LAC William Walton

Leading Aircraftsman Walton had also been posted since the Francistown hearing and his evidence was also submitted in writing. The constant posting of airmen to and from Rhodesia meant that there were no eyewitnesses available in the court to describe Adamson's and Edwards' final day:

I had refuelled Oxford HN607 on the 4th of October 1943 at Kumalo before watching Edwards and Adamson take-off at 10:45 that morning. Everything was in order and seemed normal. However, the plane did not return. I next saw the plane when I witnessed Wing Commander Grace landing it back at Kumalo on the 6th of November. I entered the aircraft and noticed that the parachute pack, the axe, the Very pistol, the compass, and the water container were all missing. These were all present when I had prepared the aircraft on the 4th of October. I never saw Edwards or Adamson again.

Prosecution Witness – Sergeant Robert Preston-Whyte

Preston-Whyte was a policeman serving with the Bechuanaland Protectorate force and was based in Francistown. Francistown was at that time little more than two main streets running parallel to and alongside the railway line to Bulawayo. However, it did sport two hotels of equally dubious nature catering for the hard-drinking types that came into town from cattle ranches or the mines that operated within the Tati concession area. Francistown had been the scene of Africa's first real gold-rush in the 1890s and, although significant deposits were never found, the town had never really shaken off its wild-west feel. Francistown was the last major railway stop on the Bechuanaland side of the Rhodesian border and is only about 130 miles from Bulawayo. The dirt road to Nata was of a similar distance, but would have taken a half a day's travelling in the 1940s. The railway provided a link for native workers from as far afield as the southern Congo to the gold mines in Johannesburg. Witwatersrand Native Labour Association (WNLA) was the leading supplier of employees to the South African gold mines and they had a transit camp at Nata that acted both as a recruitment centre and also a rest camp for those workers coming down from further north:

On the 3rd of November 1943 I left Francistown to go to the WNLA camp at Nata and, having travelled the 120 miles, I arrived in Nata at five thirty in the morning. I then proceeded to search for Twai Twai Molele who lived about seven miles out of town. I took an interpreter with me and I questioned him through my interpreter. Twai Twai said that he had seen a twin-engined aeroplane when he had been out hunting with another man at a place known as Kuaxaxa. He said he had seen the spoor of two men, but that he could not follow them due to the nature of the country. Twai Twai said he had not seen any people connected with the aeroplane.

Twai Twai then directed our lorry to a point about 25 miles north-west of Nata, about three miles south of the wet weather road to Maun. Here, on a large salt pan, we found HN607. We searched for footprints but could not find any. I examined the aircraft and found its logbook, the last entry being, 'We have gone east. Little water. No first aid. Aircraft requires petrol and oil only. Date 5.10.43. Time Zero 08:30 zero hour' signed by Gordon Edwards and Walter Adamson, 21 SFTS. I am not familiar with aeroplanes but I cannot recall seeing an axe or a water container. We returned to Nata the same day and, while not discussing any details, I asked Twai Twai to form a search party. Twai Twai said he would try. Investigations then continued.

On the 6th of December I travelled to Nekate, a small village between Nata and the pan where the aircraft was found. Although none of the women accused live there, Tammai Mashupatsela has a hut there, as does his mother. In his mother's hut we found an axe that, the natives said, belonged to Tammai. This was taken as evidence and it is in the courthouse today.

Two days later I met Rekisang, a prosecution witness, at the WNLA camp at Nata. She handed me a tobacco pouch containing eight shillings. This was made up of Rhodesian half-crowns and a South African sixpence.

On the 10th I arrested Tammai. He was wearing a pair of blood-stained khaki shorts. The blood stain was on the crotch. These shorts are exhibit L. The same day I returned to Francistown and arrested Twai Twai.

On the 5th of January, Rekisang took me to a hut in the *kraal* belonging to Twai Twai. She brought out a small bottle (exhibit F) which contained a lumpy, sticky, greasy substance along with a Rhodesian sixpence and what appeared to be human hair. The smell when the bottle was opened was revolting. On searching the hut I found Morobe (another prosecution witness) inside, very ill. I also found another bottle containing a similar sticky substance, but this time with a Rhodesian three-penny bit embedded in it. On the same day Pebane, a police messenger, brought a report of a burnt place by a water hole near where the plane had been found. He also brought an envelope containing some charred bone and cloth. I passed this straight on to Captain Langley.

On the 25th of the same month I visited this water hole on two separate occasions. The first time Rekisang took me to the spot, the second I went with Captain Langley. Rekisang pointed out a burnt patch about the size of the courthouse. It was really made up of three burnt areas, where there clearly had been a large fire as the surrounding trees were charred. The ash that remained was very fine. There was brushwood suitable for burning at the extremities of this clearing.

Preston-Whyte was cross-examined by Fraenkel, the judge, Ellenberger and the Native assessor, during which the following points were added:

When I spoke to Twai Twai at Nata I used an interpreter, although I can understand Setswana. I did not meet any of the other accused at this time. Twai Twai told us that he had first seen the missing aircraft about three weeks earlier. I travelled to the pan with five natives, including one Masarwa, and when we got to the plane the engines were covered and I did not notice if the compass was missing. Twai Twai said the spoor he had seen was of men in shoes, but that now the wind and rain had destroyed these footprints. The plane was south of the village of Kombe.

The village of Nekate consists of two 'proper' mud huts and several Masarwa-style shelters. I do not know if the handle of the axe we found there would have soaked up blood and I did not see any blood stains on it. This group of people would have done some trading and, although South African coinage is legal tender, Rhodesian money is in common use. Tammai's trousers were filthy and clearly had not been washed for a long time – the bloodstain was near the fly and was the size of a six-pence. This was the main stain on the outside of the trousers, but I noticed many various stains on the inside of the garment.

Rekisang's hut, where the bottles were found, was in the same compound as Twai Twai's. The place where she showed us the burnt patch was an area of dense scrub with no large Mopani trees, but with plenty of firewood. By the time we visited this place, Rekisang had implicated Twai Twai in the murder of the airmen.

At the end of Preston-Whyte's evidence, the native assessor for the court, Seitshiro Moshweu, expressed great surprise that Twai Twai could not have followed the airmen's footprints, given the Bushmen's legendary tracking abilities and the time of year. Justice de Beer brusquely reminded his officials that they were there only to ask questions, not to share their opinions.

Prosecution Witness – Captain Morley Robert Langley

Captain Langley was the officer in charge of the police station in Francistown and was an experienced policeman, with much knowledge of native crimes in the protectorate, having worked at almost every possible police post during his career. Unfortunately, he was in Johannesburg when news arrived that the aeroplane had been found. However, as soon as he returned he joined Preston-Whyte in Nata in order to run the investigation:

On the 8th of November 1943 I travelled to Nata and with two of my native troopers we joined a party of RAF airmen and natives from the WNLA in order to search the area around the aircraft. Twai Twai led us to where the aircraft had been and he gave me the impression that it had been there for about ten days or a fortnight. The wheel tracks of two aircraft were visible, but otherwise the search found nothing. We searched for the next few days, splitting the party with myself heading towards the

Hunters Road to Kazungula, again with no success. I returned to Francistown on the 11th and on the way organised a large search party of seventy, comprised mainly of Bangwato tribesmen. This search was also unsuccessful.

On the 14th of December I received a pair of blood stained shorts from Preston-Whyte and I forwarded these to the South African Institute of Medical Research in Johannesburg. The following week, on the 22nd, Orai took me to Kuaxaxa and made a statement and she pointed out place C on my sketch map.

On the 3rd of January I received a report from Dr Bershon that the blood on the shorts I had sent to Johannesburg was human.

On the 5th I travelled to the campsite at Kuaxaxa before arresting Tammai and Twai Twai for the murder of the two airmen. A guard was posted at the campsite until the end of the month. The following day I returned to the site of the fire near the campsite. There were still clear signs of a large fire, with nearby trees charred. There was a layer of ash about one inch deep over an area of about twenty-six by seventy-four feet. One area had been dug down to

Robert Langley (left), the lead investigative officer. At the far right is Denis Reilly who lost his life after the search for the missing RAF rugby team in the 1930s. (*John Reilly collection*)

a depth of about nine inches on the orders of Gasebalwe, a headman leading one of the search parties. On this day Preston-Whyte handed over two jars containing a fatty substance and an envelope containing bone fragments and cloth recovered from the burnt area.

On the 7th I travelled to RAF Kumalo where I was shown the possessions of the two airmen which had been taken out of storage. I checked the clothing issue cards and then took hair samples from the tunics of both pilots and also from the swimming trunks of Adamson. I also took hairbrushes belonging to each man. A week later I personally took this evidence to South Africa, with the jars containing hair and fat going to Dr Britten – the chief professional officer at the government chemical laboratory in Johannesburg, the bone fragments to Dr Macintosh – the director of the South African police medical labs, and the hair evidence to Dr Bershon.

On the 21st and 22nd of January I returned to the campsite at Kuaxaxa with Toi Toi, Morobe and Kico where they pointed out the sleeping places of their hunting party. At this point the shelters they had used were still standing, although two wooden frames that had been used for drying meat that had been present on my previous visit had gone. The shelters were rough affairs, typical of the Basarwa, made of twigs and brushwood. At this point I made a sketch of the area, A is the shelter belonging to Twai Twai and is where the airmen slept and were murdered. B was Tammai's shelter, C Morobe's, D Rekisang's, and E belonged to Keree. Temee and Toi Toi also slept in the enclosure of A. All the witnesses agreed with this layout.

I returned to this area on the 30th with Professor Macintosh and his assistant, Dr Friedman, and Detective Sergeant van Schalkwyk of the South African police, along with a party of natives. Morobe pointed out the burnt patch to us, saying that this was where the bodies of the Europeans had been burned. Van Schalkwyk took photos of the area. The following day,

I received the report from Dr Bershon identifying the hairs taken from the jar as European and similar to those on the hairbrushes taken from Kumalo. On the 31st, Dr Friedman found a Martini Henry rifle cartridge case in the area that used to be covered by Twai Twai's shelter, marked A on the map (by this time the shelters had been removed). Further searching discovered a bullet from a Martini Henry rifle about three to six inches below the surface, marked X on the map.

Although not mentioned in his evidence, after the search of the campsite, heavy rains arrived and these made the subsequent journey back to Francistown a very difficult one as the dirt tracks turned

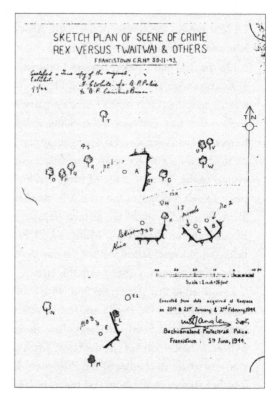

Robert Langley's hand-drawn map of the alleged murder scene.

A typical Basarwa shelter as described on Langley's map. (*Rudi Roels*)

to mud and, in some cases, mini rivers. The main party reached the Tati River bridge that led into Francistown just in time, as within an hour it had been completely inundated by the rising flood water. The unfortunate van Schalkwyk was left stranded on the wrong side of the river and had to retrace his rather damp steps the 120 miles back to Nata. An emergency plan was quickly drawn up, with the RAF offering to send a plane from Kumalo to pick him up. Instead of this, van Schalkwyk decided to risk the 130-mile drive across the top edge of the Kalahari to Maun, the centre of district government for Ngamiland, which he did successfully.

The bullet found was then taken to DS Cromhourt of the South African Criminal Bureau in Pretoria on the 7th of February. No evidence was found to confirm a definite link to the rifle we had taken possession of. On the 25th of that month I received from Dr Britten the report on the contents of the jars we had sent.

In June I produced the sketch map showing the location of the campsite. It was twenty miles direct from Nata, but it took thirty-seven miles to drive there according to the instruments in our lorries.

Lunch was then taken, one of the breaks that allowed the Basarwa legal teams an opportunity to translate what was happening in full to the defendants. On returning to the witness stand Captain Langley was first questioned by Fraenkel, who started off by asking background questions before moving onto details about how witnesses had led the police to the campsite. Langley's responses are outlined below:

I was transferred to the Bechuanaland Protectorate in November 1935 and I know the different types of natives. Twai Twai, Tammai and Keree speak 'Masarwa' and the Basarwa are semi-nomadic, spending part of the year at the cattle post and the rest of the time they spend out hunting.

I first saw the fire on the 6th of January and the road to the campsite had been used only once by a lorry, the day before when posting a guard. The local population may have known of the guard. When Morobe took me to the fire she followed the spoor of the lorry before turning off the track to lead me to the fire. Rekisang took exactly the same route.

The witnesses said the airmen slept at the southern end of the shelter marked A on the map. There was a well about 150 yards from the campsite, otherwise the nearest water would have been at Kombe. Kombe is also known as Metsebotlhoko. Bushmen need water, just like any other human being. This whole area is known as a Basarwa hunting area.

The witnesses did not show us where they had first met the white men due to the phenomenal rains.

Kelly then questioned Langley about the nature of power in relationships between men and women in Basarwa society:

Basarwa are primitive nomads and the men hold considerable power over the women and would beat them if they did not obey them. I would agree that women would have no choice but to fetch water if asked and that they would probably cover up hunting by hiding skins. Again, I would agree that the women would have carried the bodies of the airmen if ordered. They are simple people and obey their lord and masters.

At this point there was a brief discussion of marital coercion where it was confirmed that only Kiree and Anchere were actually married. De Beer then asked about Twai Twai and hunting:

Preston-Whyte was the first to interview Twai Twai, as I was away from Francistown when the first reports came in. Twai Twai was the head of the hunting party as well as the head of his village, but I do not know how far his power extends. As the head of the party he would have been in charge of where to go and what to shoot, he also would have been in charge of the distribution of the meat. We found only giraffe legs and heads at the campsite, not a whole skeleton. We also found a number of places where giraffe had been shot, but some bones had always been removed – although the heads were usually left.

Prosecution Witness – Dr Britten

The next witness for the prosecution was Dr Britten, who had forensically inspected the jars found that contained hair and fat. He had made the journey from the Government Chemical Laboratories in Johannesburg, where he was the Chief Professional Officer. At that time these labs were under the jurisdiction of the Department of Agriculture and Forestry:

I received two jars on the 13th January 1944. One jar contained a mixture of fatty material, starchy material and hairs along with a sixpence coin. The fat was mainly animal but was mixed with a mineral fat of some type. The other jar had similar contents except there was also some twigs and the coin was a thre'penny bit. The mixture of fat in the second jar was predominately mineral with some animal fat, the other way round to the first. Due to the mixing of the fats it is very difficult to isolate individual components so I cannot give a firm opinion on whether the animal fat was human. The piece of cloth I received in an envelope was a piece of felt. I cannot say whether this could be linked to the gun or the casing.

Prosecution Witness – Temee

The final witness of the opening day of the trial was the one that everybody had been waiting for, especially the gathered press corps. Temee was the first of the Basarwa hunting party to give evidence and so was the first witness to describe in detail what had happened to the missing airmen. This was done through two interpreters, the first translating to Setswana and the second from Setswana to English. Temee was still only 16 years old at the time of the trial:

I am Temee, the son of Resetora and Micke. Keree is my uncle, but I am not related to Twai Twai or Tammai. At the beginning of the summer I went with Tammai and Keree as part of a hunting party and we met with Twai Twai's group at Kuaxaxa. All of the accused were part of this enlarged party.

On the 4th of October I was at Kuaxaxa when I saw a plane fly over in the late afternoon. We were all at the camp, although Twai Twai, Tammai and Keree were taking the donkeys to the well when this happened. We all slept at the campsite at Kuaxaxa. At daybreak the following morning we heard the aeroplane's engines. Twai Twai, Orai, Toi Toi, Tammai and myself went to look for the aeroplane. We all travelled on donkeys except for Tammai who used the horse. We found the aeroplane on open ground near the pan, but, although there was spoor, there was nobody there. We decided to follow the spoor and we came across two white men just before we reached the village of Ramatamoli. There was a tall man and a short man.

Temee was then asked to describe in detail what the men were wearing and carrying. This took some time and it became obvious that Temee, or the interpreters, did not have words for all that he wanted to say. Descriptions of colours and materials involved pointing at various people wearing similar items in the courthouse. The description of the jackets was particularly problematic as it could not be made clear whether Temee was referring to shirts and jackets or vests and shirts. This must be remembered when reading the next section, where repetition and confusion have been removed:

The tall man had a hat with metal on – like a button or a badge – the hat was like the WNLA peaked caps, it was khaki in colour. The tall man had long trousers on and the short man was wearing shorts, both men were wearing a shirt and a jacket. One of the men had a mark on his arm like the soldiers wear. One of the men was carrying an axe, it was an unusual axe with a hole in the head. That was all I saw the men carrying.

We took them to the campsite at Kuaxaxa and they rode there using the horse and one of our donkeys. It was in the afternoon when we returned to the camp. When we got there we gave the white men giraffe meat to eat but they did not eat it.

That night the white men settled down to sleep first, they went to bed in Twai Twai's shelter. The rest of us men and some of the women stayed around the fire longer. While we were around the fire, Twai Twai suggested that we should kill the white men so we did not get into trouble for killing the giraffes. Tammai agreed with Twai Twai. Tammai and Keree were next to go to bed. I went to sleep in Twai Twai's enclosure along with Orai, Toi Toi, Twai Twai and the two airmen. Keree lived with Autwa, Morobe and Chikawe stayed in another shelter, and the three other women all slept in Rekisang's shelter.

I was lying down but was not fast asleep when I saw Twai Twai stand up and then Tammai arrived with a Martini Henry rifle that he normally kept in his shelter. Twai Twai had his muzzle loader. Twai Twai shot one man and he died. Tammai shot the other man but he struggled so Tammai took his axe and used the sharp end on him to kill him. Blood came out and stained Tammai's trousers. By this time Keree had arrived and the noise of the shooting brought the women too. Twai Twai and Tammai then took the boots off the two airmen and then Twai Twai ordered Keree to help him carry the tall man's body away. Tammai told the women to help him carry the other body, so Anchere and Haukwe helped him and Keree to carry the short man away. They carried the bodies into the bush in the direction of Cutico. I stayed in the camp and saw Morobe come back to carry some coals, then I saw a big fire in the direction they had carried the bodies.

The next morning, just as it was getting light, the women came back into the camp. Chenda was carrying some of the white men's clothes, including a shirt and a pair of short trousers. She told me that they had burnt the bodies. Orai, Twai Twai and Tammai then returned from the direction of last night's fire. Twai Twai brought with him hair from the bodies and he was also carrying the white man's genitals. That morning, the party left the campsite with Bene, Anchere, Autwa and Haukwe going to Cutico and the rest of the party going to Kombe. Twai Twai and Tammai carried the possessions taken from the white men with Twai Twai having a shirt, a pair of shoes, trousers, jacket, and a hat. Tammai took with him the axe from the airmen, shoes, trousers and a shirt. I never saw a water container.

Tammai gave some white material to Chenda to make a dress. This material had been carried by the white men in a bundle fastened with a red belt. This material was a large amount. I saw Chenda wear this dress, but she hid it when Captain Langley arrived in a lorry and I never saw it again. I did see the airman's axe at Nekate with Tammai. I also know that Matammai (Tammai's mother) kept one of the pairs of trousers belonging to the airmen. Tammai turned the trousers he was wearing at the time of the murder into shorts. These trousers had blood on them.

This dramatic evidence brought the first day to a close. As Justice de Beer adjourned for the day, the press hurried away to wire the latest developments around the Commonwealth and the prisoners were taken across the courtyard, back to the cells.

TUESDAY 26 SEPTEMBER

With news of Temee's evidence being the talk of the whole country, it was no surprise that the crowd surrounding the courthouse was even larger the following day. Before the case started for the day all the court's windows were opened wide, giving some opportunity to those straining to hear the proceedings from outside. Temee was back on the stand, under oath, to face his cross-examination. As usual, Fraenkel was first up. He walked Temee through the evidence he had given the previous afternoon before questioning him on the clothing and appearance of the airmen:

The short man was wearing shorts and had on black shoes. I cannot describe his socks, but they were not black or brown. This was the man who was carrying the axe. The tall man wore brown shoes and had black socks. He carried the material with a belt around it. Both men wore shirts and jackets.

The questioning then moved to the events at Kuaxaxa:

We arrived back at the campsite at about four or five o'clock. When it got dark the white men went to go and sleep. They took off their hats, but did not undress. I do not know if they took their shoes off but they kept their axe next to them. The belt from the material was removed and the white men slept on the material. The coals of the fire were still alive when the rest of us went to bed.

The first shot woke me up and I saw Tammai take the second shot. I know Twai Twai fired the first shot because there was still smoke coming from his gun. This was the gun he had shot a *kudu* with, before we found the white men. I did not see the wounds, but I saw blood over Tammai's clothing. There was lots of blood when Tammai used the axe on the back of the white man's neck. By this time the women had arrived. When the bodies were carried away the socks and shoes had been removed. I never went to the fire. When Twai Twai came back he was carrying dark hair – this included part of the scalp.

Finally, the questions turned to the events after the murder:

The clothes of the airmen were clean; I did not notice any blood on them. These clothes were shared out at Jaire before the party split up. The material that was given to Chenda was the material I saw the white men with. After the dress was made, Tammai had the material that was left over. I did not see Tammai hide anything before the police lorries came. Tammai did cut his own trousers down to shorts, but this was because they were old and had been torn riding. The police never beat me to make me say these things.

Kelly then asked very brief questions about the events at the fire before Temee had slept:

Only Twai Twai, Tammai and Keree were involved in the conversation about what to do with the white men, but when I went to bed I knew murder would be done.

The prosecution then re-questioned Temee to clear up some points:

When I woke up I saw Twai Twai stood over the tall white man with his gun just discharged. I did not see any blood or a hole in the white man's clothing. There was blood on the floor of the shelter. Twai Twai had shot a *kudu* with this gun, but this was many days before. Tammai had used his gun to kill a giraffe a couple of days before. The meat in the camp was dried meat, or *biltong*, from this giraffe. The animals had been shot from the horse.

Tammai changed the handle of his axe later because it had broken in the murder.

The court then confirmed that Temee had stayed in Nata after the murder and also asked him to clarify some of the relationships in the hunting party. Temee said that Chancha was concubine to Tammai, Keree was Chenda's brother and that Keree was married to the sister of Anchere. Finally, Temee described the piece of white material he had seen as being about 10 feet long, but this was when it was folded.

Prosecution Witness – Rekisang

Perhaps surprisingly, the next witness was the daughter of the main accused. Rekisang had decided to turn King's Evidence against her father, Twai Twai, who she still lived with. She too was a member of the party that had been illegally hunting giraffe at the time of the pilots' disappearance:

> I was part of a hunting party that started from Nata. I travelled with Twai Twai, Toi Toi and Kitso to Nekate where we met Tammai's group. Tammai was travelling with Morobe, Temee, Chikawe and Resetora. From Nekate we went to Kuaxaxa where we were joined by Keree. Keree had Autwa and Orai with him.
>
> On the 4th of October 1943 I saw an aeroplane flying towards the east. At this time the three hunting parties were together as one. Later that day Bene, Chenda and Anchere joined us. The next morning we heard the aeroplane and Twai Twai, Tammai, Orai and Toi Toi left the campsite on the horse and donkeys.

Later that day, they returned with two white men in soldiers uniform. They were both wearing shorts and shirts, and both shirts had badges on the arms with stripes on them. They only had shirts and not jackets. They were carrying an axe with a black handle, like the one in the court.

That night I heard Tammai and Twai Twai discussing what to do. Twai Twai asked Tammai, 'As you have brought these white men here, what are you going to do with them?' Tammai replied that he did not know what they could do with them. I thought they were talking about taking the white men home. Keree was present at the fire when this conversation happened and must have heard, but he said nothing. Twai Twai then said, as they were on the veld, they should just murder the white men and take their money off them. Tammai agreed. This happened around the camp fire, the white men had gone to Twai Twai's shelter, but I do not think they were asleep. After this everyone went to sleep in their respective shelters.

At night I heard and I saw Tammai pass by with a rifle in his hand on his way to Twai Twai's shelter. Keree also went to Twai Twai's. I saw Twai Twai with a rifle in his hand, he had shot the tall man. Tammai then shot the other man and when he still struggled he passed his gun to Keree and he took his own axe and hit the shorter man on the back of the neck. This axe stayed in Twai Twai's shelter. I could not see what the white men were sleeping on as I was too far away, but I could see that they had slept in their clothes and then I saw Twai Twai take their shoes off. Twai Twai and Tammai then carried away the body of the tall man with help from Bene. Keree was told by Tammai to help carry the bodies, Keree did not object but he had to be ordered to carry the short man. Keree was helped to carry by Chenda and myself.

At this point lunch was taken for the second day, once again giving a hurried opportunity for the defence to explain to the accused what had happened over the course of the morning. This was an easier task

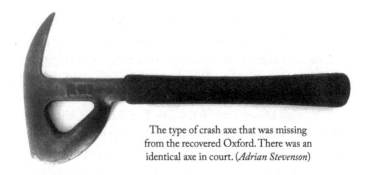

The type of crash axe that was missing
from the recovered Oxford. There was an
identical axe in court. (*Adrian Stevenson*)

due to the fact that that the defendants could at least understand all
of Rekisang's responses. Rekisang then started the afternoon session
by describing the immediate aftermath of the murders:

> We carried the bodies to the place that I had pointed out to
> the police. Twai Twai and Tammai undressed one body each
> before they cut off the private parts. Twai Twai then removed
> the hair from his body. I did not see Tammai remove any hair
> but I did see him remove fat from the loin of his body. This fat,
> along with the hair and genitals, were the only parts that were
> removed. Twai Twai and Tammai then cut the bodies into bits,
> starting by cutting them in half at the waist and then chop-
> ping the legs off. I saw blood on the floor where this was done.
> All the women helped by collecting wood, Keree only helped
> by putting the wood into the fire. Tammai ordered Autwa to
> bring coals from the campsite so that he could light the fire.
> The bodies were then burnt. When the bodies were fully burned
> and there was only some bones left, I went back to the camp
> with the women. Orai, Tammai, Twai Twai and Keree stayed
> at the fire for a while longer. Twai Twai had made a parcel of
> the hair and fat using leafs and branches, I carried this back
> to the campsite. Chenda carried the fat Tammai had cut out.
> The other women carried nothing.

The men arrived back after sunrise and Twai Twai and Tammai carried with them the white men's clothes as well as the private parts. Twai Twai took the fat off me and melted it with zinc over a fire, when it was melted he added the hair to the mixture and then poured the liquid into a bottle. Some medicine and a sixpence was added to the bottle. At first I thought Twai Twai had got the sixpence from his hunting, but then I thought he must have taken it from the white men as I had not seen it before. The bottle is the one in the court today.

Finally, Rekisang described what happened as the hunting party broke up:

At Kombe, Twai Twai gave me the bottle of fat with the sixpence in. He told me that I should put it on my face, but I do not think that Masarwa women can be made beautiful by fat and medicine so I did not use it. This was the bottle I later gave to Preston-Whyte, the policeman. Morobe had another bottle of fat, but I am not sure where she got this from – she will be able to tell you that.

We stayed one night at Kombe and then I went to Methlomoganyane with Tammai and Chenda. Tammai gave Chenda some white silky material that she made herself a dress from. I first saw this material in Chenda's shelter at Kuaxaxa, the one she shared with Tammai, as we were getting ready to leave. This was the first time I had seen it.

After two nights at Methlomoganyane we went to Jarie for a couple of days. At Jarie, Twai Twai gave me nine shillings in loose coins that I put into my bag. The coins were all silver and some were foreign. I gave this money to Mr Batty.

Mr Batty was part of the British South African Police group that had helped with the search for the missing pilots. Despite their name, this was the police force for Southern Rhodesia and they had offered full assistance with the investigation. When Rekisang handed the money over there was only 8*s* in the purse:

> I am sure that Twai Twai had no money when we left Nata to go hunting. Twai Twai was with us at Jarie and this was where the white men's clothes were divided. I watched this from the shelter I was using, about twenty feet away (6 metres), and I could see the items come out of a box, including the water container that Tammai took. I could not see any bloodstains on the clothing from where I was.

Fraenkel was again the first to cross-examine the witness and as usual went through the timeline before going into greater detail, this time starting with what happened after the group left Jarie. As Rekisang described the journey back to Nata, this approach ran into a problem those with no experience of the region could have expected:

> It took days to get back to Nata from Jarie and then many days later the police came.

Fraenkel wanted to know how many days, but the best answer Rekisang could give was 'many'. This led to a short confrontation as Fraenkel tried to tie down a fixed date (how many days? how many weeks?) and it appeared that the witness was being deliberately obtuse. The translator then came to Rekisang's aid by explaining to the court that 'Rekisang cannot answer as Masarwa do not know how many days in a week'. Fraenkel then changed tack by going back to the events on the day of the alleged murder:

> The party that went out to search for the aeroplane left before sunrise and returned around midday. The white men they found were both wearing khaki shorts although they wore different colour socks.

There was another break at this point as finding translations for colours was very problematic. Khaki was dealt with by pointing to a uniform in the courthouse, but describing the exact colours of the socks proved too much and the detail was left unknown. Fraenkel was forced to change tack again and immediately ran into more linguistic problems as he tried to tease out whether Rekisang was asleep at the time of the first shot:

> At the time of the murder the fire near Twai Twai's shelter had died down and there were no flames, but the coals were still red. I was not asleep but lying on the ground when people went to bed. I was not fully asleep at the time of the first shot.

This final point took nearly five minutes of questioning to establish as the translator could not find the necessary words to differentiate between lying down, being asleep, being awake and getting up:

> The tall man was shot in the neck, the other man in the ribs. The men were undressed in the bush near the new fire and they both had vests on. The socks and shoes were left at the camp. Temee stayed in the camp and he was just waking when we returned, though he was fully awake when the men returned. I only saw hair cut from the white men, I did not see any skin with it. I did not see the private parts after they were brought back to the camp. The material I saw in Tammai's shelter was folded – I know there was enough to make one dress. Twai Twai packed up that morning, putting all the clothing in one bag that was strapped to a donkey. Tammai and Twai Twai took one hat each at Jarie – I did not see any blood on the hats.

Perhaps surprisingly, given the detailed story Rekisang had told the court, Kelly decided not to ask any questions of this witness. Instead the court officials tried to clarify various points. Twice they

returned to the issue of whether Rekisang was awake at the time of
the first shot. After much to and fro with translations, the following
was the final position:

> There was no moon that night. I saw Tammai and Keree go to
> Twai Twai's shelter before the first shot, so I was only half asleep
> at the time of the shooting. There was very little time between
> the two shots fired. Even though the men had talked about this
> around the fire I did not think that it would actually happen.
> Temee, Toi Toi and Orai were so frightened that they ran away
> straight after the shooting. The man who was shot through the
> ribs bled a lot, I carried his legs. I had only seen animals shot
> right through before. I did not notice blood on his clothes, only
> on the ground. When we got to the place of the fire the bodies
> were cut up using a knife and Tammai's axe. Tammai had gotten
> blood on his trousers, near the fly. Keree was not wearing trou-
> sers or a shirt and so he had no bloodstains. I only noticed blood
> on the white men's clothes when they were folded up later on.
>
> Afterwards, Twai Twai gave the money to me as his mother
> would have wanted a proper explanation as to where it had come
> from. His mother was not home when we returned so we took
> the clothes to Twai Twai's second wife, Dambe. The bottle with
> the fat was used to carry Vaseline, but it was empty at the time of
> the murder. My evidence is not affected by my religious beliefs.

The mention of Dambe must have raised a question in Fraenkel's
mind as he then asked Rekisang about the relationship between
them. Rekisang explained that Twai Twai preferred Dambe to
Rekisang's mother and that her mother had argued with Twai Twai
and Dambe over this, but that this quarrel had not influenced her
evidence. Rekisang claimed that she had always been on good terms
with her father and this was shown by the fact she lived in the same
small village as him, even after the killing.

Rekisang's evidence had taken up most of the second day and the judge called an overnight halt at this point. The mention of medicine and the strange mutilation of the bodies, especially of the genitals, certainly excited the press as it offered an exciting alternative to illegal hunting as a motive for the alleged murders. This was reflected not only in the following day's papers, but also in some of the persistent rumours that built up around the case.

WEDNESDAY 27 SEPTEMBER

Prosecution Witness –
Morobe

The third day was opened by another daughter of the main accused. This time it was Morobe who was giving evidence that could potentially see her father, Tammai, hanged. Her evidence was almost identical to Rekisang's, describing how an aeroplane had been seen flying east on the fourth and then heard again the next morning. She told of how a search party had been sent out with the horse and donkeys, and of how they had returned with two white men. We pick up her story as she sat around the fire after the two airmen had retired to Twai Twai's shelter:

> I heard Twai Twai say 'Let us kill the white men' and Tammai agree to the suggestion, but I did not hear what else was said afterwards. I was surprised by this conversation, I did not think they were serious. I really did not think they would murder the white men.
>
> After the shooting, the bodies were carried away towards Cutico, but the white men's socks and shoes were left at the camp. The other clothes were taken off by Twai Twai and Tammai at the fire that they were making to burn the bodies. Tammai ordered me to get the coals from the campsite to light the fire, which I did. At the fire I saw Twai Twai take fat from under the ribs of one of the bodies. Keree helped collect the firewood.
>
> I was back at the campsite before sunrise, though it was just getting light. Rekisang and Chenda carried the clothes back

to the campsite. I saw blood on those carried by Chenda, but I could not see the clothes that Rekisang took.

The body parts, including the fat and the genitals, were burnt and the mixture collected in two bottles. This medicine would help the owner to have good luck and get more money. Tammai gave me his bottle to look after for him, I did not use it.

When we left, Tammai took the airmen's axe. At this time Tammai was wearing long trousers that he later made into shorts. I did not see any bloodstains on these trousers. I saw a water container that he had got from the white men. It was like the containers I have seen in stores. Tammai also took some material that I later saw being made into a dress. This material was not big enough. I also saw two blankets that had belonged to the airmen.

The latter had been referred to as 'pieces of material' during the Francistown hearing and this was pointed out to the court as the judge had the pre-hearing transcript in front of him during the trial. This was the first of three points where Morobe's evidence to the court differed from her previous testimony, leaving the court to decide on whether these discrepancies were translation errors, honest mistakes or something more sinister. Fraenkel then started his cross-examination by focusing on points of detail:

The tall white man had black hair, while the short man had light coloured hair. I think the white men were asleep when I went to my shelter to sleep. After the shots were fired Twai Twai and Tammai called the women together. The tall man had been shot in the head, by the left temple – there was lots of blood. The short man had been shot in the loin but he also had a wound by his ribs. It was the tall man that was still struggling. When the bodies were undressed, only one man was wearing a vest. I saw some bloodstains on the clothes, but there was only a little blood on the clothes belonging to the tall man.

There was then some confusion over which women had carried what back from the fire, again there was some difference between Morobe's evidence and her earlier recollections. The next question produced the final change from her earlier testimony at Francistown:

> Twai Twai took the water container I had seen.
>
> I do not know how long it was before the police arrived because I do not know how to count days.

This time Kelly did take the opportunity to question the witness. He kept the questions short, focusing on the state of mind of the women involved:

> The white men had left to go and sleep by the time Twai Twai talked about killing them. I have never seen anybody killed before, so I did not take this conversation seriously. When the murders happened we were alarmed and afraid, we only carried the bodies because we were ordered to. We knew it was wrong but we were too frightened to run away. In any case, it was dark and there was nowhere to run to.

The Attorney General then took the opportunity to ask further questions of his witness:

> When the bodies were being undressed the fire had already been lit, but it was still small and I could only see a short distance. I only saw one side of the man who had been shot in the head. I saw where the bullet went in, making a wound of about two inches. I saw a wound on the neck of the man that had been killed with the axe. I could see this, but I did not touch the bodies. I did carry the fire from the campsite, but I refused to help carry the bodies.
>
> When the police came Matammai, Tammai's mother, took the items that Tammai had himself taken from the two white men.

Ellenberger and Mackenzie, the two District Commissioners, then took their respective turns with the witness:

> The white men took their shoes off before sleeping. The blankets they used were white, but a different colour to the dress that Chenda made. The white men had carried these blankets into the camp. The water container they brought had a string to carry it, it was not like our water containers because ours are made of animal skin. The men slept on their left-hand side.

Mackenzie pointed out that if they had been sleeping on their left then the tall man could not have been shot in the left temple. He asked Morobe how this was possible:

> I did not see the right-hand side of this man. The other man had two wounds. At the fire the bodies had their arms cut off at the elbow and the heads removed.

Prosecution Witness – Toi Toi

Following a lunch break, the prosecution called Toi Toi as their next witness. Toi Toi was part of the party that had gone to search for the aeroplane when it had been heard on the second morning. He started by explaining his relationship to the other members of the hunting party, perhaps to the consternation of his translator:

> I am the son of Resetora and Keree is my uncle. Chikawe is my sister and I am related to Tammai, but this relationship is too complicated to explain.
> I was one of the party that went to search for the white men. We found the aeroplane first and then we followed the white

men's tracks until we found them. When we got to the white men they were carrying an axe and a suitcase made of red leather. The case had a handle.

The description of the suitcase was made by Toi Toi initially pointing to a dispatch case in the court. He then used a photograph of a parachute pack to identify it as such:

I later saw white material inside this case. The men also had a canvas water container.

The white men went to sleep in their clothes and with their shoes on. I went to rest in the compound of the same shelter. In this shelter there was Orai, Twai Twai, Achube, Temee and a small boy, Luayo. I did not hear any conversation about killing the white men. When the shots were fired Keree was still at the fire.

When the bodies were carried away only their hats stayed in the camp, the shoes were brought back later by Chenda. I did not go to the fire where the bodies had been taken to, but it was a big fire and I could see it from the campsite. When Rekisang came back she brought with her a package of black hair tied together with bark. Twai Twai and Tammai brought back some fat and the white men's private parts. Keree did not carry anything back from the fire.

After the killing, I saw Tammai with a watch. At Mothlomoganyane, Twai Twai told us all to conceal everything and not to talk to anybody about what had happened. This was said in front of Tammai.

Fraenkel started his cross-examination by accusing Toi Toi of previously claiming that he had been beaten by the search party organised by Preston-Whyte after the aeroplane had been discovered:

The search party asked us all for information about the missing white men. I refused to give then any information, but I was not beaten.

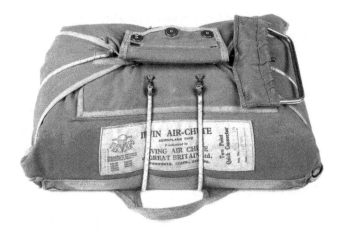

The type of parachute pack that Adamson would have worn.
(*RAF Museum Collection – PC98/173/5885/21*)

This suggestion of coercion was to become more important later on, but for the moment Fraenkel was happy to go back to the details around the time of the alleged murder:

> We had been at Kuaxaxa a long time, but I cannot count the days we were there. When we found the white men, the tall one was wearing long trousers with black shoes. He had dark hair. The short man had yellow hair and he also had on a pair of shorts with brown shoes. One of the men was wearing a watch, I cannot remember which one. The case they were carrying had metal catches, but I never touched it.
>
> The men slept in their shoes and I remember that they were still wearing them when the bodies were carried away. The fire outside of Twai Twai's shelter still had some flames, but I was too far away to see the wounds that were inflicted. When the bodies were moved I went to the spot where they had been killed. The case, the hats, and two pieces of material had been left in the shelter – the shoes were not there. The hats had peaks on them.

The description of the hats depended on a lot of translation and eventually by the court asking Toi Toi to pick out a similar hat in the courthouse:

> The next morning I left the campsite briefly to collect the donkeys. This was from not far away, about the same distance as the grass outside the courthouse. I did not see the fat being burnt, but I did see the clothes being packed into Twai Twai and Tammai's bags. I later saw the white material from the suitcase at Kombe, it was enough to make one dress.

Kelly then again kept his questions short, only picking up on a couple of detailed points:

> On the morning after the killing I also took the donkeys to get water from the well, this was about 150 yards away from the campsite. Afterwards, I saw Twai Twai with a piece of the white material from the suitcase.

The court then took the opportunity to confirm some of the details from the earlier hearing in Francistown:

> Tammai's Martini Henry rifle was not very reliable. It often had to be taken apart each time it was fired, but this could be done quickly. I did see blood on both sets of clothes brought back from the big fire.

Prosecution Witness –
Kico

The final witness of the third day was yet another relative of the main accused, Kico being the niece of Twai Twai. She was a member of the hunting party that had gathered at Kuaxaxa. Her evidence was probably the vaguest of the prosecution witnesses, with very little actually having been seen:

> I was not a member of the party that went to look for the white men and only saw the Europeans when they were brought back to the campsite. When they arrived one of the white men was carrying an axe. This was the only thing I saw them carrying.
>
> I was too far away to see the murders clearly, but the tall man stopped struggling after he was hit with the blunt side of the axe. This was Tammai's axe and was normally kept in the kgotla.
>
> After the murder I saw Tammai and Twai Twai share out the money they had taken from the white men. This happened at Jarie. I did not see any water container. I know I told the District Commissioner at Francistown that I had seen this, but I only did this because I was afraid of the DC. This was the first time I had been in trouble and was scared, but Rekisang had told me what to say.

With this intriguing admission the court was adjourned for the day.

THURSDAY 28 SEPTEMBER

Given the previous day ending with the current witness, Kico, admitting that she had lied under oath at the previous hearing, it was no surprise that this was where Fraenkel started his questioning:

> I did not see the water container, but Rekisang said that I should mention this when I was in the court. I told Rekisang that this was not the truth, but I was frightened of District Commissioner. This was the only time I did not tell the truth in Francistown.

Fraenkel then turned to events around the actual killing. Again it proved that the word that was being translated as being asleep could have a range of meanings and, despite several persistent attempts, the defence lawyer could not pin down whether Kico was awake or not at the time of the first shot. Kico appeared to claim to have both been asleep and to have seen Twai Twai fire the first shot. Finally, Fraenkel looked at the issue of the pilots' clothing:

> The two white men were both wearing shorts. When the clothes were shared out I did not see any vests or shoes. I did not see any hats either.

Fraenkel pointed out that Kico had claimed that she had said that she had seen the airmen wearing two different types of hat when they arrived in the camp. Kico responded by saying that she could not remember. Kelly again declined to question this witness and it was left to Ellenberger to ask why Tammai would give the silk from the parachute to Chenda. He also then asked why Kico had lied in Francistown:

The police station opposite the court, where the accused would have spent their breaks. (*Botswana Aviation Art*)

> Tammai gave Chenda the material to make a dress because he always gave everything to Chenda. Rekisang did not tell me to say that I had seen the water container, she only told me to say 'yes' if I was asked whether I had seen it. I only did this because I was frightened.

Judge de Beer then walked Kico through all the inconsistencies in her evidence compared with the testimony in the pre-trial hearing in Francistown. Kico claimed that the story told to this court was the correct version of events and that she had been mistaken at Francistown. The judge then worked hard over several questions to establish that Kico was lying down, but not asleep, at the time of the first shot. Once this was apparently settled, the native assessor asked a final question to which Kico responded that she was asleep when the first shot was fired – leaving the court little wiser.

The final prosecution witness was then called.

Prosecution Witness –
Awekeca Resetora

Awekeca was married to Resetora and was his fourth wife, polygamy being both common and accepted. Resetora was the father of
Temee, Toi Toi and Chenda, all of whom were part of the hunting
party and heavily implicated in the case. Despite them not being
biologically hers, Awekeca considered them to be her children.
Awekeca was the only prosecution witness not to have been at the
scene of the alleged murder and her story started when the news of
the killing reached her:

> When we heard about the murder, Resetora said we should go
> to the children straight away. We went straight to Kombe and
> there we found Tammai, Matammai, Bene and Chenda. Inside
> of Tammai's hut I noticed an axe with a black handle. It was not
> like a native axe. We stayed one night at Kombe before return-
> ing to Nekate. As soon as we got home a police lorry arrived
> from Kombe and the police took Tammai, Temee, Chenda and
> Morobe with them. Bene and Matammai were not taken by
> the police and they came to live in Nekate. Matammai brought
> the strange axe with her when she came. I know this because
> Matammai's hut had collapsed and she was staying in Dambe's
> hut while Dambe was away. I saw the black-handled axe hidden
> in the rafters of Dambe's hut.

Fraenkel began his cross-examination by asking Awekeca how she
felt when the others were arrested:

> I remember the day they were arrested as it was raining heavily
> and I was very upset. When we were in Kombe, Tammai shared a
> hut with Chenda as she is his concubine. I do not know how long
> this was after the murder as we Masarwa never know how long.

At Nekate there was a leather bag in Dambe's hut, but I did not look in it. I was with my husband, Resetora, and my small child, Chara, when I saw this bag. I do not know who brought the axe that I saw, but it arrived at the same time as Matammai. I did not see anything else in the hut. By this time, Tammai and Twai Twai had been arrested.

With Kelly again declining to question the witness, it was up to Ellenberger and Mackenzie to add more detail to Awekeca's account:

At Kombe there are four huts and these belong to Dambe, Matammai, Chenda and Morobe. Matammai is also the mother of Autwa, one of the accused women.

I do not remember Preston-Whyte coming to look for an axe. I did not know Tammai's axe before I was shown it in court, but my daughter Chicawe did know it and pointed it out to the police. I did not tell the police about the axe in the rafters when they first came because I had not seen it then. Chicawe knew about this axe, but was too afraid to tell anybody. Chicawe lives with me and our hut is about a mile from Dambe's.

Prosecution Witness – Flight Lieutenant Ronald Payne (Recalled)

After hearing all of the prosecution witnesses, Flight Lieutenant Payne was recalled to clear up various issues that had come to light during the course of the trial so far. The RAF officer from Kumalo had been asked back to go through various technical descriptions, starting with items that were missing from the aircraft:

The missing parachute pack was of the observer's type and was only clipped to the body before use; normally it would be stored in the aircraft during flight. The pack was a canvas box with metal framing. The framing would collapse as the parachute was pulled out. The container was secured with red bands, that is the elastic was white, but the bands had red cotton threads running through them. It would have weighed about thirteen pounds. The canopy was a single piece of silk and was worth about eighty pounds. Because of this cost it is unlikely the airmen would have damaged the parachute by cutting it, although it is standard practice to use it for sleeping in an emergency. No blankets were carried in the aircraft.

The water container that should have been in the plane was a metal cylinder about eighteen inches by nine and would have held two gallons of water. It did not have a handle. The bands that secured this were still in place in the aircraft when it returned to Kumalo. There are no standard canvas water containers that are issued by the RAF, but the pilots might have carried their own. There was no clock in the aircraft and I do not know if one of the pilots had a watch, but the time on the note they left was specific. The missing compass was about the size of an alarm clock.

The Oxford carried two signalling strips, about eight feet long by eighteen inches wide. These are made from white oil cloth and are used to signal to aircraft from the ground. Along with the two strips there are five metal discs with holes in them. These allow a range of messages to be sent. These had been placed out on the ground, but it was impossible to say how they had been set up as they had been blown out of place by the wind. The two strips had been blown about the length of the aircraft, around fifteen feet.

The questions then turned to the physical description of Edwards and Adamson. This was important as the prosecution witnesses had all described Edwards as tall and dark-haired, where Payne, in his initial evidence, had described his hair as 'fair'.

Adamson had dark hair and weighed about one hundred and fifty pounds, Edwards weighed somewhere between one-seventy and one hundred and eighty. Edwards had fair hair, but he used brilliantine and this could make it look darker. They would have worn leather flying helmets. I am convinced of this because the leads for the microphone were left in the plane and the pilots had contacted ground control after they had took off. They would have been unlikely to have carried any other headgear unless it was very hot or sunny – the Oxford has an enclosed cockpit but the glass lets the heat of the sun's rays through very easily. The two pilots had peaked caps, but would only have used these for 'walking out' and it would have been very unusual for them to have taken them with them in the air.

Brilliantine was a popular hair product, originally from France, and was very similar to Brylcreem. The lack of eyewitnesses that could describe the men was compounded by the fact no photographs of the deceased were available to the court.

Finally, the Attorney General asked to submit the statements the accused had made in the pre-trial hearing as evidence. He outlined that while Twai Twai and Tammai denied everything, the other defendants had described events pretty much as the prosecution had painted them. The Attorney General suggested that these documents should be translated for the benefit of the defendants. Fraenkel objected to this approach as there had been no chance of any cross-examination in the Francistown court. The Attorney General claimed that the defendants had not asked to, while Fraenkel claimed they were not given the opportunity to ask. The judge stepped in and accepted the statements and this closed the prosecution case. However, de Beer asked for the recall of Morobe so he could ask her about Kico's allegations that she had encouraged Kico to give false evidence. The judge also asked about why the other witnesses claimed that she had carried some of the

murdered airmen's clothes back from the fire, something she had
denied in her testimony.

Prosecution Witness –
Morobe

> I never spoke to Kico at all and never told her to change her
> evidence. Nor did I carry any clothes belonging to the white men.
> The other witnesses are telling lies.
>
> At the time of the murder I was very afraid. I asked my father
> 'Why are those people being killed?' Twai Twai replied 'What are
> they to you, to ask such a question?'

This brief exchange brought the morning's proceedings to a close
and lunch was called. The courthouse slowly emptied, with many
of those leaving wondering what defence Twai Twai Molele would
employ after the recess.

Defence Witness –
Twai Twai Molele (First Accused)

Twai Twai cut an impressive figure as he stood before the court.
Six feet tall, Molele gave off an air of power such that the whole
court was aware of the strength of his personality. His grizzled face
and bald head may have told that his 50 years had been hard ones,
but his deep-set eyes, looking out from under heavy eyebrows, suggested that he was in full control of his thoughts:

> I am Twai Twai Molele and I live at Nata with my wife, Dambe.
> Last year I went to Kombe and then to Kuaxaxa to hunt. I went
> with Tammai, Temme, Rekisang, Toi Toi, Kico, Selatole, Chikawe,

and some of the children. We were at Kuaxaxa for about a month and Keree joined us during that time.

One day, while out hunting, I came across an aeroplane on the ground. This was the first time I had seen this aeroplane – I had not seen the aeroplane in the air. There were five of us out hunting that day, there was me, Tammai, Temee, Orai and Toi Toi. We were on our way back to the campsite when we found the plane. I did not see any people or any tracks near the aeroplane. It had been there a long time and there had been a fire and the ground was burnt. There had also been a lot of wind. We went back to our camp. We did not see any white men, any axe, and we did not have any visitors at the campsite. We did not take anything from the aeroplane.

The next day we went hunting again – Keree, Toi Toi, Tammai, Temee and me – and this time we killed a *kudu*. I had with me my muzzle loader, Tammai used his Martini Henry. The following day we went back to the kill to collect more meat. We then left the campsite and I went with Tammai, Rekisang, Temee, Toi Toi, Kico, Chicawe and Seltole to Mothlomogyane. We spent two days there and then one night at Jarie. We then split up and it took me two days to get back to Nata. I returned only with my blankets, I did not have anything that was not mine. When we got back I reported the aeroplane to Rre Mareke at the WNLA camp at Nata. This was the day after I got to Nata – I had slept first.

About five days later I saw Preston-Whyte, the policeman. I took this man to the aeroplane and he asked me to organise a search party, but I was arrested before I could do this. I told the policeman that I could not find any spoor around the aeroplane.

I had never seen a European axe until I saw it in the court. This was the same with the bottles of fat, I had never seen them and I never owned one either.

Twai Twai's denial of almost everything, except being a member of the hunting party that had found the missing aeroplane, came as no surprise to those that had been present at the Francistown hearing. With only minor changes in detail, this was the story the head-man had told since his arrest. It was now up to Attorney General E.R. Roper to try and find any chinks in Twai Twai's story. His first point of attack was Twai Twai's relationship with his daughters, two of the lead prosecution witnesses:

> Rekisang is my daughter, but we are not on good terms because she always takes the side of her mother. This is the only reason for her hatred. I live in the same village as her mother, but I do not always treat her mother well. I do not know whether her mother would tell the police about this. Despite all of this, I do treat Rekisang well.
>
> Morobe is also my daughter, but we are always on good terms with each other. Her mother is Mamorobe, who is now married to one of my sons.

Many in the court would have liked to have a detailed family tree of the Molele family in front of them in order to try to follow the intricacies of some of the twisted branches. Roper, however, seemed to take this in his stride and next moved onto Twai Twai's friend-ship with the other members of the hunting party, all of whom seemed to have some family connection:

> Temee and Toi Toi are sons of Resetora. I am on good terms with them, but I do not get on with their father. Toi Toi's mother is now my wife – that is why I took the boys with me. Kico is the daughter of Meche, my cousin who is now dead. I treat Kico well. Of all the party, there was only Rekisang I was not on good terms with.

Roper then turned to the inconsistencies between Twai Twai's account of finding the aeroplane and that which had already been heard from the prosecution witnesses that had been part of the search party:

Despite what Preston-Whyte said, I never told the police that I had seen footprints. I would have noticed any prints if they were there. Temee was lying when he said he saw spoor, I would have tried to trace them if we had found any. Toi Toi is also wrong. If anybody had seen any footprints he would have shown them to everybody else. Perhaps somebody did see some footprints, but I did not and they did not show them to me. I do not know why the boys would lie about this.

I did see the signal cloths, there were two pieces of material and some metal discs. This cloth had been blown around. We did not touch anything and we took nothing with us when we left. We did not see any people, the boys made this up. I do not know why they did this; perhaps they wanted to get me into to trouble, so they did not. Maybe they made it up because lots of people were asking about the aeroplane and they were afraid of the chief. There is no evidence against me. I can only be convicted on what they say.

Finally, Roper asked about the bottle of fat and the money Rekisang had claimed Twai Twai had given her:

I never gave Rekisang any money, perhaps her husband did. She got the bottle and the money from her husband. She told me her husband gave her money when we were hunting. We left this money at home when we went to Kuaxaxa. Rekisang's husband is a person of Rhodesia so he ought to have money from Rhodesia. This money was for a dress, her husband left it when he went back to work in Johannesburg. Rekisang is lying about the bottle. All the witnesses know it was hers.

Fraenkel then took control of his witness again, asking why the boys would give evidence so damning against a family member. Twai Twai ensured that the idea of a conspiracy entered the mind of the court:

There are people behind the boys. They were threatened by the chief. Keree heard this at Francistown.

Although not mentioned by name, it appeared that Twai Twai and Fraenkel were suggesting that Tshekedi Khama had used his men to apply pressure to the witnesses. Kelly was up next and satisfied himself by confirming that Twai Twai fully understood the charges he was faced with and the seriousness of the alleged murder. The two District Commissioners then had a chance to question the alleged ring-leader. Ellenberger asked for more detail on what had happened when the plane was found, questioning why it took so long to report the finding of the aeroplane:

> I looked at the aeroplane carefully, but I stayed on one side of it. I did not go close and I did not see a door. Because of this, I wondered how the men had got out. The tracks of the aeroplane went some distance. I noticed this when we were looking for the spoor of the men. I reported this within ten days. I know that according to the law it should have been reported, but I was hungry and had to hunt. I was also frightened of what would happen.

Ellenberger argued that it was twelve days and used Twai Twai's evidence to show this. Twai Twai disputed this and there was a short discussion on this point before Mackenzie took over. Ellenberger's opposite number checked that the grass where the aeroplane had landed was already burnt before the arrival of the aircraft and Twai Twai agreed this was the case. The native assessor then challenged Twai Twai over how they could be hungry after the kudu hunt and also why his children would give evidence against him:

> The *kudu* we shot after we saw the plane was a small beast and there was not enough meat for everybody so we were still hungry. The children want us in trouble as the Masarwa are full of hatred.

Nothing but hatred exists amongst the Masarwa. I have never before heard of children testifying against their father.

The assessor also suggested that it should not have taken two days to return to Nata as Kuaxaxa was only 37 miles away. The Attorney General finished the examination of the main accused by asking about his knowledge of aeroplanes:

I have seen an aeroplane before on the ground. This was at Serowe. I do not know how people get out of an aeroplane.

And with that the powerful healer was replaced by the contrasting Tammai.

Defence Witness – Tammai Mashupatsela (Second Accused)

Whereas Twai Twai had impressed the court with his height and presence, Tammai was short and stocky, and had a more obvious 'Bushman' appearance, with his lighter skin and prominent cheekbones. He was clearly much younger than the man he had just exchanged places with. Fraenkel walked him through his story, sticking to the main points. Like Twai Twai, Tammai's defence was that they had never even seen the missing pilots, let alone murdered them:

We were out hunting when we came across an aeroplane. This was around midday. I only saw the plane from the back and one side, there were no people there. We did not shoot anything that day and we returned to our camp. The native axe and the Martini Henry rifle in the court are mine. There is a problem loading and firing that rifle – sometimes I have to fire five bullets before it fires properly.

Four days later I left to go to Kombe. I never saw any white men or their possessions. While I was at Kombe, Resetora visited my hut. I remember that day because it was raining so heavily. My bag was in the hut and inside were an adze, a rasp, three knives and some brains. The brains were animal brains. There was no axe. I did not see any other axe in Matammai's hut in Nekate.

Fraenkel then asked his witness about the mysterious bottles of fat, and Tammai offered a new and alternative explanation for them:

The bottle of fat was mine. I had bought them from Patsima, who is a witchdoctor in Nonga. I kept them at my home and I used them on my face to bring me good luck and money. My brother and Rekisang know this, because they had also bought the same.

Tammai almost certainly meant his sister and this was probably a mistake on the part of the translator. Even today many Setswana speakers use 'he' and 'she' interchangeably when speaking in English. Roper's first questions were about the strange bottle, starting with how the money got to be in the container:

I put the threepence in the bottle on the instruction of Patsima, as the witchdoctor had no money. This coin was part of the change I got when I bought some tobacco in Nonga. Patsima told me the medicine would bring me lots of women and also would mean I would get assistance from my people when I needed it. The witchdoctor told me the coin had to be a thre'penny bit, but it did not have to be Rhodesian. Talifang also bought a bottle.

The Attorney General then asked why Patsima had not been mentioned as the source of the bottles earlier and why he had not been produced in court as a witness:

Patsima is too far away for the police to bring him here. I did not force him to come to give evidence as I have no power here. I did mention Patsima in the Francistown hearing.

Roper was not impressed with this response and pointed out that Patsima could have easily been brought to the court if Tammai or his attorney had asked for him. The interrogation then moved onto Tammai's friendships with some of the witnesses and their reasons for giving evidence in the trial:

I had left my bottle at home and I was surprised that the children gave it to the police. I think Morobe lied to the police about the bottle because she was in trouble or was told to do so by other Masarwa. Morobe is my step-daughter and I have always treated her well. Rekisang acted the way she did because of the hatred that exists between the Masarwa, especially between her and her father. Rekisang is my uncle's daughter and she hates me because of the hatred between my father and her.

Temee only gave evidence because he was ill-treated by the search party. The same goes for Toi Toi and Kico. I heard they were all thrashed by the Bangwato.

Resetora is still my friend. I think she only talked about the axe because she had heard rumours that the police were looking for one. My mother will confirm there was only an adze, not an axe, in the hut.

An adze is an instrument very similar to an axe, but the cutting edge, instead of being parallel with, is perpendicular to the handle. It is fair to say that someone not familiar with them would today describe them both as axes. Roper next asked about Tammai's actions when the plane was found:

I did not look all around the aeroplane as I did not want to disturb the ground and any possible footprints.

Roper then pushed the point, asking what 'all around' the aircraft meant and how did he expect to find footprints without a proper search. Tammai then changed his story slightly:

> We did go all around the aeroplane, but we did not go to the engines. Twai Twai also walked all around the aircraft until we were sure there were no footprints. The aeroplane had been there a long time so all the spoor had disappeared. The others only told of any footprints after they were mistreated.

Finally, Roper asked about the blood on Tammai's trousers that had later been turned into shorts. Tammai initially claimed it was animal blood from when he was hunting, but when Roper used the South African lab report to refute this Tammai said that the blood was his. The blood was there from when he was sick.

Fraenkel then used this opportunity to clarify a few points of his witness' evidence. This was limited to three areas:

> The trousers were last washed at Nekate, long before the hunting trip.
>
> We did walk all around the aeroplane looking for spoor.
>
> Resetora is still alive, but he has given no evidence either here or in Francistown.

The various officers of the court then took their chance to question Tammai's account. Mackenzie wanted to know how Tammai could have had change from buying tobacco when Tammai claimed to have no money. Tammai explained that he had sent somebody with meat to barter for the tobacco. The other questions related to finding the aeroplane:

> I never left the hunting party while we were at Kuaxaxa so I can say that nobody heard the aeroplane. The first time we saw it was on the ground after it had landed.

FRIDAY 29 SEPTEMBER

Defence Witness –
Keree Oitube (Third Accused)

The last of Fraenkel's charges to give evidence was Keree. Another young man, he was tall and dark-skinned like Twai Twai, but there the similarity ended. Keree had much less force behind his personality and had spent much of the trial either day-dreaming or drawing animals. This doodling of elephants, giraffes and impala, scratched out either on the floor or on his own arm using matchsticks, had earned him the nickname of 'the artist' among the watching press.

He had given some strange and contradictory evidence in the Francistown hearing, where he seemed to be angling towards giving King's Evidence. This would be a key part of the prosecution cross-examination. However, Keree would start his testimony with a very brief outline of what had happened on the hunting trip:

> Twai Twai and Tammai are my fathers-in-law. When they were out hunting they found an aeroplane. I was not with them and did not see the aircraft. I did not see any white men, any clothing, or an axe on this trip. After they had seen the plane I went to my home at Cutico.
>
> Later, a messenger from the chief came to ask me to show him where the white men were. He was very angry and told Sergeant Preston-Whyte to arrest us. Preston-Whyte thrashed me and Orai. The others were also thrashed.

At this Roper objected, pointing out that this had not been mentioned before. The judge agreed that this point should have been brought up earlier, preferably when Preston-Whyte was on the stand. Certainly Preston-Whyte or Captain Langley should have been made aware of the allegations. Despite what had just been translated, Fraenkel claimed that he was not sure who had committed the beatings and he was allowed to re-question his witness:

> I do not know the name of the sergeant who beat me, but it was the one who came from Francistown. Before that I was beaten by Xewema, a Masarwa who was part of the search party. He wanted me to show him where the white men Twai Twai and Tammai had murdered were. The chief's messenger told me that Xewema was also a policeman. My father was also thrashed by him. I did not actually see any of the other witnesses beaten, but I heard about it.

Roper started his examination of Keree by asking about Keree's relationship with the other defendants and by pointing out that it is impossible to have two fathers-in-law, something Keree was adamant about:

> I do have two fathers-in-law for I am married to their daughter, Autwa. I am related also to Toi Toi, Morobe, Rekisang, and Temee. I have always been on good terms with them all.

Given this, Roper then asked why they would give evidence against him.

> Temee and Rekisang were told what to say. I don't know why, but I do know that Ramestane, the chief's messenger, told Rekisang what to say.

Roper then moved onto what happened when the aeroplane was found. It must be remembered that Keree was the only one of the main defendants, and the only male accused, not to have been part of the party that found the aeroplane:

I spoke to Temee and Orai when they returned; they came back just before Twai Twai and Tammai returned. They said they had found an aeroplane, but there were no men with it. They both said they had seen footprints though.

I asked Twai Twai and Tammai about this. They said they had not seen any prints, but they were old men and perhaps the young boys had better eyesight.

Temee and Orai lied about finding the white men because they were thrashed.

The court then moved onto perhaps the strangest piece of evidence presented in the case. During the hearing in front of Mr Midgely, the District Commissioner in Francistown, Keree had made a bizarre statement telling of a dream that he had had. The statement was made while Keree was under arrest and despite warnings that he did not have to say anything and that his statement could be used in evidence against him. Roper got Keree to confirm his earlier evidence:

There is a dream that I believe is also a lie, that we murdered two white men. There was myself with Twai Twai and Tammai, along with Temee and Toi Toi. I dreamt that Twai Twai had a gun and he shot one white man through the chest. The other white man was pierced by an assegai through the ribs and was finished off with an axe. Temee was the one with the axe in my dream, Tammai had the axe. My dream came true, as confirmed by Tammai a few days ago.

Roper then asked if Keree stood by what he had said:

I dreamt it like that, but it was Twai Twai that confirmed it, not Tammai. I had this dream while I was in the police cell. Twai Twai said it was true because I had dreamt it. Twai Twai then told me all about the murder, he wanted to know why I had been arrested because it was him that had done the killing and now lots of people had been arrested. I told him I was arrested because of Rekisang and what she had said. He told me that the white men had been shot with their own rifles and that one had been finished off with an axe. Twai Twai told me he had given his rifle to Temee to hold and then he had used the axe. I never held the rifle.

Roper then asked if the story about the dream had been thought up by Keree in order to escape his responsibility for the crime. Keree gave an astonishing one word answer:

Yes.

Keree's seemingly contradictory testimony led to a lengthy discussion as to what the court should consider to be his evidence. Judge de Beer was understandably confused by the fact that when initially giving evidence he had not seen any white men, but then the details of the murder are described in a 'dream'. The confusion only grows as more of the original dream is read out to the court in which Keree describes Twai Twai and Tammai bringing the airmen back to the camp on a horse and a donkey. The statement continues by describing the murder and how Twai Twai's gun did not work and how he had to use a spear instead; he then includes details of cutting up the bodies and the disposal of the remains by the act of throwing them down a well. Keree is asked what he meant by the phrase 'How the white men suffered'.

I said that because their deaths made me sad and because I was worried. I did not see them suffer though as I was away watering the donkeys and I only heard one shot. I got the full story from Twai Twai when we were in a cell together in Francistown.

When they were searching for the aeroplane there was one nice sergeant. He spoke to me kindly and treated me well, but the other police spoilt this.

Roper then asked about other parts of the dream, to which Keree responded with a rambling statement:

> Twai Twai, Tammai and Rekisang told me to say the bodies were carried a long way. Tammai told me the bodies had been carried on horses before being cut up and put in the well. I did not see this, my conscience tells me. No, I got this from Tammai, not my conscience. Tammai said Twai Twai cut the bodies up, but Twai Twai said both of them did it.

When Roper accuses Keree of telling three different stories at different times, Keree blames the District Commissioner:

> The DC, he told me to hold back some information for the next hearing. He told me to make a surprise in the big court.

Faced with such perplexing statements, the court then spent some minutes discussing what to make of them. Roper suggested the statement described Keree's own lightly disguised actions and was an attempt to plead King's Evidence in the earlier hearing. The judge expressed some sympathy with this point of view, but could not reconcile this with other witness statements – especially the part about disposing the bodies in a well. Roper then asked why the statement was made, why the plane was not reported, and whether Xewema had really beaten him:

> I was insane at the time I made the statement. I did not kill anybody, it is Twai Twai and Tammai that are the murderers. The object of the statement was to exculpate myself.
>
> I did not report the plane because I did not see it myself. I did not resist when Xewema asked me to go with him.

With his witness now telling a very different one to that with which he had opened it was up to Fraenkel to rescue what he could from the situation as he again took charge of Keree's evidence:

I sometimes go insane and I dream a lot, but my dreams, they never come true. When I made this statement it was with a native trooper and one of the interpreters in the court today. I was told a European would speak for me at the trial. I cannot tell which parts of my dream are true as I got a lot of the information from other people. In my statement I did say, 'Twai Twai and Tammai are not worried; they are fit and did the murdering ... Twai Twai and Tammai are Tshekedi's equals, and Khama becomes their dog.'

The police did not ask me to show them the aeroplane as the children had already shown them. I did go once to the plane with the police when I was at Nata.

The bizarre reference to Tshekedi Khama would be contested later on, but, if true, it certainly gave some idea of how the Basarwa in that region thought about Khama. Keree ended his turn on the stand with a couple of questions from the District Commissioners that added little.

Defence Witness –
Matammai

Despite having given statements in the Francistown hearing, Kelly had decided not to put any of his female defendants in the witness box. Indeed, Kelly had obviously decided that there was simply not enough evidence to convict his charges of murder and was content not to call any further witnesses at all. Fraenkel on the other hand felt the need to use Tammai's mother as his third from last witness:

My name is Tabe, but everybody knows me as Matammai because I am Tammai's mother. Although I live at Nekate, I was at Kombe when the hunting party returned. I remember Tammai unloading his donkey. I did not see anything unusual, no clothing, and no strange case. At Kombe, Tammai shared his hut with Chanda.

I remember the police coming in the lorry because of the heavy rain. Awekeca was there when they arrived. I know Tammai's bag, it was there in his hut that day. There was nothing in the bag. Nothing not belonging to Tammai, that is. His adze and rasp were in there. I never saw the axe belonging to the airmen.

Next we went to Nekate, I did not share a hut there with Dambe. I recognise the medicine bottle in the court – it belonged to Tammai. He has had it for three years. There was nothing left in it, but it used to have a white mixture that Tammai would put on his face. There was a thre'penny bit in the bottle. I do not know the place it came from, although I had heard its name.

Roper asked for a further description of the mysterious medicine bottle:

The mixture was a watery medicine that Tammai rubbed between his eyes. He used it about once a month. He got it from Nonga. Tammai told me this three years ago. I do not know who else bought this medicine, but it was definitely three years ago. This is the fourth year.

Given the earlier evidence about Basarwa having difficulty counting days, Roper asked repeatedly how Matammai could know it was three years ago. Matammai could not explain so Roper moved onto Tammai's bag and the axe Awekeca had seen in Dambe's hut:

The bag was a skin one that Tammai had used many times. I just happened to look in that day and I saw the brains and tobacco Keree had brought. I was getting tobacco from the bag and I saw nothing else in there. I was first asked about this bag by a policeman from Rhodesia. He emptied it and only found tobacco. Tammai kept his adze in that bag usually, it was in the bag that day.

I am not related to Awekeca and I understand that she says she saw an axe, but I did not. I slept in Dambe's hut with Talifang and Awekeca is making a false statement about seeing an axe in the rafters there or at least if she saw an axe there, I did not.

Matammai was then asked for clarification of certain points by the officers of the court:

Tammai had only one bag, although he had a smaller one inside that he used to keep cartridges in. I know these were not there when the bag was searched, but Tammai did not give me or our daughter anything to look after.

I was using Dambe's hut as mine had fallen down. It is not true that I pulled it down when I heard of the murder. In fact it was Batty, the Rhodesian policeman, who told us to pull it down so we could build a new one.

I know the bottle came from Patsima, but I did not know Patsima was a witchdoctor.

Finally, Roper asked about Matammai's statement in Francistown where she had claimed Keree's father had given the airmen's axe to Letsami, Twai Twai's brother, to hide:

I only said that to get Letsami into trouble.

This was the first mention of Twai Twai's brother during the trial, although he would feature dramatically in the aftermath of the judgement.

Defence Witness – Mamorobe

The penultimate defence witness was Mamorobe, Marobe's mother. Although Morobe was Twai Twai's child, Mamorobe was at that time living as Tammai's wife, or, in the more accurate language of the time, his concubine. 'Tickey' was South African slang at the time for threepenny bit:

> I know Tammai. I live with him in Nekate. Tammai had gotten the medicine bottle from the village of Matidzi. Tammai told me about Patsima when he bought the bottle. He has had one bottle for two years, perhaps this is the fourth year. Inside the bottle was fat, hair from a white man, and a tickey – I saw this when Tammai brought the bottle home the first time. He used to smear the fat on his face, but he did nothing with the tickey.

The Attorney General was quick to point out that Matidzi was a long way from Nonga, where Tammai had claimed the bottle had been bought. Roper then asked for more detail on the strange contents of the bottle:

> I do not know where Matidzi is, although I know Nonga. The hair in the bottle was European; it was very different to our hair and it was white. The fat was thin and greasy, almost like water. He smeared it on his face and, when it was empty, Morobe's husband came with more fat. This was Vaseline, and this was all that was in the bottle when Tammai left it with me when they went hunting. The white sergeant took it when the bottle was in Rekisang's hut. It had been taken from Morobe when she was ill in Rekisang's hut. The hair and the threepence were still in the jar then.

The native assessor again picked up on the discrepancy in the description of where the bottle had been bought:

> Tammai got the bottle from Nonga. I have never been there and I do not know the place.

Defence Witness –
Talifang

Fraenkel's final witness was Talifang, who Tammai had claimed had bought a medicine bottle at the same time as him:

> I live at Nekate and I know Tammai well. I know the bottle Tammai had, but it is not one of the ones in court. He got his bottle in Nonga from Patsima three or four years ago. I was not present when he bought it. The mixture had hair and threepence in it and it was contained in a Vaseline bottle.

As with Matammai, Roper wanted to know how Talifang knew it was three or four years, especially when the court had been told that Basarwa could not count days:

> This is the fourth year because we have ploughed three times since. I am Masarwa and, although we do not count days exactly, we know the seasons.

After asking whether Talifang had discussed the case with anyone, Roper turned back to the bottle and its contents:

> I have not discussed the case with anybody, including Mamorobe. Patsima had a big bottle of fat, this is where the fat in Tammai's came from. I can now see the bottles here in the court, one of those bottles is mine. The bottle with sixpence in was Rekisang's and the one with thre'pence was Tammai's. The hair in the bottle was definitely European and white. I know because I have seen it on their heads. There was red medicine in the bottle too. The whole mixture was watery enough to see the hair was white, even in the bottle.
>
> I had my bottle for three years and Tammai bought his from Patsima at the same time. I kept my bottle in Matammai's basket

and Tammai kept his in a pair of socks at Mamorobe's. Matammai never kept Tammai's bottle, it was always with Mamorobe.

The final question of the defence witnesses was asked by Mackenzie, the District Commissioner. This was to shed light on whether Talifang was actually present when Tammai bought his bottle:

> I was in Nonga when Tammai bought his bottle, but I was not present because I was at the Kgotla. Tammai put the money in the bottle himself.

Although technically Talifang was the last defence witness, Fraenkel took the opportunity to recall Sergeant Preston-Whyte in order to cast doubt on Keree's testimony. This was despite the fact that Fraenkel was Keree's attorney.

Witness –
Sergeant Robert Preston-Whyte

Preston-Whyte was asked about the well where Keree had suggested the remains had been hidden:

> We searched the well thoroughly. It is about two hundred yards from the campsite at Kuaxaxa and it is about fifteen feet deep. We had to remove sediment before we collected more water from the well. We did not find any human remains.

And with this last piece of evidence the defence rested their case and lunch was taken, ready for the start of the summing-up in the afternoon.

SUMMARY OF THE CASE FOR THE PROSECUTION

The Attorney General decided to split his summing-up into two distinct parts, choosing to deal with the five women accused before moving onto the men who were at the centre of the alleged crime.

Roper started by stating that, with the exception of Temee's evidence, all the witnesses placed the women in their shelters at the time of the discussion between Twai Twai and Tammai, when the murder of the airmen was decided. This meant that the only evidence against the five was that they had helped dispose of the bodies. In view of this, Roper asked for a verdict of being accessories after the fact to the murder.

All of the five had made statements in Francistown that corroborated the prosecution case and Roper now presented examples of these to the court. Bene, the fourth accused, had described how she had arrived at Kuaxaxa on the day the search party left to look for the aeroplane and how this party had returned to the campsite with two white men. During that night, she was woken by the sound of rifle shots and was too afraid to go and look, but was told that the white men were dead and that she had to help carry the bodies. Her statement then went on to describe how the bodies were burnt and how the possessions were shared out. Finally, she told of how the dress, water container, and axe that Tammai had kept were hidden when the police arrived at Nekate. The other four had told very similar stories, although the details were not read out in court.

Next, Roper turned to the point of culpability. The main issue here was whether the women had acted under compulsion. The Attorney General's claim was that while the women were told to move the bodies, they were not threatened into doing so. This led to a discussion of where this stood in contemporary law. Roper claimed that marital compulsion did not apply to the case, as none of the accused were formally married and that customary marriage should not count. The judge, de Beer, disagreed with this point and also suggested to Roper that a command by a chief, holding power of life and death, was sufficient excuse and likened this to a soldier acting under orders. The Attorney General claimed this was not relevant and, without a specific threat attached, a simple request to move the bodies was not sufficient reason to absolve the accused.

The judge then used Captain Langley's evidence that 'these people are in a wild and semi-nomadic state ... where the men have considerable power over the women; that they beat them for diso-bedience; and that orders were implicitly obeyed' to suggest that an active threat did indeed exist. Roper responded by pointing out that the latter points applied, perhaps to a lesser extent, to European women and that 'One hears of wife beating ... it has not died out in all classes of society', but this does not excuse the women. He argued that the law must be applied consistently across society and that none of the women had claimed to feel threatened when they gave their evidence. Not even Autwa, who was customarily married to Keree, had claimed any compulsion from her husband.

Having dealt with the women, Roper now moved onto the main accused, Twai Twai, Tammai and the dreamer, Keree. The Attorney General began by outlining the prosecution case against the three men and where the evidence against them had come from.

Starting with Temee and Toi Toi's evidence describing the search party and the finding of the missing airmen, through Rekisang's, Morobe's and Kico's recounting of the airmen returning to the camp and being offered the giraffe meat, to the recalling of the conversation where Twai Twai and Tammai discussed the killing of the missing pilots, Roper gave a clear account of who had said what and reminded the court that giraffe were considered royal game.

Before moving onto the actual murders, Roper looked at possible motives. He pointed out that while the only motive to come out in evidence was the covering up of the illegal giraffe hunting, there were other possible reasons. Roper suggested the airmen may have been killed for their belongings, their money or for *muti* or medicine. He claimed that in crimes of this sort there is rarely a single motive, but rather a combination of several.

Returning to the actual crime, the Attorney General then walked the court through the killings as described by Temee, Rekisang, Morobe, Toi Toi and Kico, admitting that there was some discrepancy over which body was finished off with the axe. Morobe and Kico had told the court it was the tall man, but the other witnesses had said that it was the shorter man who had survived the initial gunshot and was struggling on the floor until the axe fell. Roper retold the burning of the bodies and suggested that only Kico, Rekisang and Morobe had told of the rendering down of the fat taken from the bodies, as the younger members of the group were attending to the donkeys at the time.

Turning to the evidence of the main accused, Roper pointed out that it simply consisted of a flat denial of the events described in court and a claim that the prosecution evidence was nothing more than fabrication. Given this accusation, Roper then went through his witnesses looking for possible reasons for them giving false evidence.

The brothers Temee and Toi Toi were the first to be considered, with Roper explaining that they were related to Twai Twai and Tammai as well as Chenda, who was their sister. The boys were on good terms with the accused and there was nothing to suggest their evidence was influenced by ill-will.

Kico and Morobe were also dealt with briefly, before Roper turned to Rekisang, who Tammai and Twai Twai had both accused of lying because of the treatment her mother had received from the two men. Roper suggested to the court that if this hatred existed then it would have been unlikely that Rekisang would have been invited on the hunting trip. He also tried to suggest that Rekisang had claimed not to see blood on the clothes in order to minimise her part in the murder, perhaps subconsciously as she had made no bones over carrying the hair and fat back from the fire. Roper also admitted it was likely that Rekisang had discussed what had happened with others, probably including Kico, as most witnesses to an event like this would. This did not mean she had tried to influence Kico's evidence.

The biggest problem in the prosecution case was the inconsistency in small details and it was this Roper addressed next. While admitting discrepancies in the descriptions of the pilots' clothing, Roper offered a suggestion that the pilots could well have taken peaked caps with them to protect them against the sun, especially given the heavily glazed cockpit of the Oxford. The different description around details of the murder, such as who had carried what, could be explained by the extreme circumstances, claimed the Attorney General. Indeed, when people had been woken in the middle of a moonless night by gunshots and had found a shocking murder had been committed, it would have been very extraordinary if there had been no discrepancies.

Roper then moved onto what had happened to the possessions of the airmen, starting with the axe that was missing from the aeroplane. He pointed out the descriptions of the axe matched the type that was missing and that most of the witnesses claimed Tammai had taken possession of it. Awekeca had seen this axe in Tammai's skin bag, before later seeing it hidden in the rafters. It was unlikely that she would confuse this unusual axe with the differently shaped adze. Roper then cast doubt on Matammai's evidence, recalling how she had claimed the bag was empty before changing her mind in the next sentence. He also found it suspicious that Matammai would remember a specific occasion of looking for tobacco when she would have done this on a regular basis. He also pointed out that Matammai had originally claimed to have seen the axe and that when the police came she said it had been given to Letsami, Twai Twai's brother, for safe keeping.

The water container that was missing was Roper's next problem as the witnesses had not described the missing large cylindrical object with any accuracy. The Attorney General put forward the idea that the container may have been removed from the aircraft after the murder and that the airmen had said in their logbook note that they had 'little water'. Roper's idea was that they would have taken what water they had with them, but that they might have used personal water containers to do this.

The parachute was dealt with next, with Roper emphasising that at least some of it had ended up as a dress for Chenda before it was hidden when the police came. The watch Toi Toi had claimed to have seen Tammai with must have come from the airmen as they had left an exact time on their note. The money Rekisang had was clearly not from her husband, Roper said, for if her husband had given her such money she surely would have bought a dress rather than using it to give false evidence. The fact that her currency matched that of the Rhodesian coins in the pots of fat was strong corroboration of the prosecution's tale.

It was then pointed out that none of the witnesses had described the Very pistol or the compass and that these were also missing from the aircraft. Roper took this to support his theory that somebody had been to the aircraft during the month it sat on the pan and taken anything of value, including the water container.

The Attorney General then returned to the jars of fat, referring to the fact that the lab report confirmed the presence of animal, possibly human, fat mixed with other substances. He then rubbished the defence witnesses' explanations as to where these jars had originated from. Matammai saying the bottle was empty and nothing but Vaseline was added, but changing her story later to say the hair and coin had been there all along. Talfang's evidence had been 'contradictory' and 'confused', especially the fact that she could tell the colour of the hair inside the bottle, despite the fact the Vaseline in her bottle was supposedly red.

Roper then provided a possible explanation for the lack of bones, inferring that Twai Twai and Tammai had opportunity to dispose of them, both after the women returned to camp when the bodies had been burnt and the men had returned a short time later, and also when the two men had separated from the group returning to Kombe for several hours to 'go hunting'.

Twai Twai and Tammai's evidence was then considered in detail, with Roper casting doubt on not only their denials but also picking up on the inconsistencies. One of the main areas was around the timing of the finding of the plane, with Twai Twai and Tammai having told the court it had been there a long time, yet this was impossible, even though it would account for the lack of spoor. The fact they had been in the area and not heard the plane was also odd, Roper thought.

Roper finished his summing-up of these two witnesses by putting it to judge de Beer that the prosecution witnesses were consistent in their story and they had no reason to lie. If the court was convinced the airmen had reached the campsite then the rest of the case followed. Justice de Beer then pointed out that this simply reduced the case to a question of the credibility of the two sides. The Attorney General agreed this was so.

Finally, Roper assessed the final male defendant, the decidedly odd Keree. He pointed out the similarities in Keree's rambling statement and the prosecution case and puts it to the court that Keree had wanted to give King's Evidence and so gave an incomplete account that minimised his role. Keree, Roper asserted, was present at the murder even if he did not take part in the attack – perhaps due to the fact there were only two guns.

His final summation was:

For all of these reasons I submit, my Lord, that the Crown has proved its case against not only against the five women accused of being accessories after the fact of this murder, but also against Nos. 1, 2, and 3 accused that they actually carried it out, and if Keree did not take a share in the killing of the deceased he was at least an accessory after the fact.

SUMMARY OF THE CASE FOR THE DEFENCE: KELLY

With his clients now facing the lesser charge of 'accessory after the fact', Kelly was given the first opportunity to speak for the defence and for the five women whose future depended on his presentation. At the end of a long week, a hot and dusty Friday afternoon is perhaps not what the lawyer would have wished for.

Kelly had been placed in a difficult position by his clients' statements in the Francistown hearing, for they effectively were a confession to the crime they were now accused of. As Roper had stressed during his summing-up, these statements confirmed all the main points of the prosecution case. To ensure the court was aware of the limitations this imposed on his defence, Kelly read from Gardiner and Lansdown (*Criminal Law and Procedure*, volume 1, page 230 – this book was effectively the bible of criminal law in South Africa), outlining that ethically he could only argue that there was insufficient evidence for a conviction or take advantage of any exception which might relieve the accused from criminal responsibility.

Kelly's first argument was a simple one, as Roper had admitted that the only charge his clients could face was accessories after the fact of murder. If there was insufficient evidence to convict the men of murder then it would be impossible to charge the women. His second, and slightly contradictory argument, was that while there was evidence that the women had helped move the bodies and brought firewood to help remove traces of the crime, the charge of accessories was the most they could face. He then used the case of *Rex v. Mloi* as an example of where a native had helped to dispose of a murder victim, but had been excused completely.

The next argument employed was that of coercion. Kelly referred to the earlier description of the Basarwa as 'rude, semi-nomadic, uncivilised' and claimed that womenfolk of such races are subject to the whims and orders of not only their husbands but of men in general. At this point Justice de Beer asked if Kelly thought a specific threat needed to be made. Kelly advanced the idea that the fear of reprisal was there, even without a further threat. Furthermore, this threat of reprisal was covered by law, as according to Gardiner and Lansdown the coerced party does not need to be married but just to have a domestic relationship in order to diminish responsibility. Kelly contended that the extended family relationships of the hunting party constituted such a situation. Morobe's evidence that the women were 'ordered' to help and, according to Rekisang, Keree was also told to carry the bodies, was evidence of coercion. The fact that Keree, a man, was forced to help, showed how much more pressure would be upon the women, Kelly asked.

Kelly finished his submission by conceding that his clients had confessed to the crime, but that they were acting under orders and were being coerced, even if they were not verbally threatened. This should be taken into account when punishment was dispensed. Kelly suggested that the nine months the women had spent in gaol was already sufficient penalty if the defendants were found guilty.

As Kelly rested his defence, the Attorney General rose to his feet and raised a point of law. Using page eighty of Gardiner and Lansdown as a guide, Roper reasoned that while the presence of a husband could imply a threat and reduce complicity, it did not completely excuse a woman of her actions. Using *Rex v. Kybers*, a case from the Orange Free State, de Beer stated that the presence of a husband could indeed constitute a threat, and that this threat was magnified in a primitive society where a woman could be expected to be chastised if she did not comply with her husband. Kelly ended this discussion by pointing out that there was not just the presence of the males, but that there were definite orders given.

SUMMARY OF THE CASE FOR THE DEFENCE: FRAENKEL

The court was very aware that the case was keeping many important people tied up in tiny Lobatsi. The District Commissioners needed to return to the north, various other officials to Mafeking, and of course Justice de Beer himself was on secondment from South Africa. This meant that Saturday morning saw the court reconvened and Fraenkel on his feet giving his closing address.

While Kelly's defendants faced a lengthy time in jail at the very worst, the three men Fraenkel was representing faced the ultimate sanction and this must have preyed on the lawyer's mind as he rose to address the court.

The defence counsel raised three issues that were the basis of his coming arguments. First, Fraenkel suggested that the prosecution had failed to provide sufficient evidence of the death of the two airmen. Next, he raised doubts as to whether the airmen supposedly killed were actually Edwards and Adamson before asking whether, even if there had been a murder, there was sufficient evidence to link his defendants to it.

Before looking at each of these points in detail, Fraenkel drew the court's attention to the fact that his clients are people 'that are the most primitive and least civilised south of the equator, and perhaps the whole of Africa, people with a very low mentality and to whom perhaps life and the truth is very cheap indeed'. He then contrasted their smart European appearance for the court with the minimal garments they would have worn normally. The suggestion that his own clients were sub-normal beings may have been an unusual technique, and today would have been seen as racist nonsense, but Fraenkel then used this idea to suggest that the Crown witnesses may have been told to tell a simple story. This story, he claimed, was that the two airmen had been found, murdered and burnt. This would be simple enough for the Basarwa to remember, but it would also explain the inconsistencies in the prosecution evidence. These inconsistencies included the description of the airmen, their clothes, their hats and what they were carrying when they were found.

Fraenkel pointed out that while the majority of witnesses described the airmen as having a water container, none of these descriptions matched the article missing from the aeroplane. He contrasted the description of the size of the parachute material the witnesses had given with that of the RAF evidence and admitted that if Chenda's alleged dress had been found it would have been fatal to his case. But it had not. Some of the witnesses had described two pieces of material, and Fraenkel declared that the airmen would never have cut the parachute, knowing its value. The missing axe, he went on, was never found and that it was easy for the witnesses to point in court to a type of axe they had never seen, and this could not prove the identity of anything. Finally, Fraenkel pointed out that not one scrap of clothing or other material had been found, and there was nothing to identify the alleged victims as Adamson and Edwards.

Fraenkel then moved on to the evidence produced by individual witnesses, starting with the scientific evidence. Dr Bersohn could only say the hair was probably European, Fraenkel emphasising the 'probably'. Dr Mackintosh had told the court that after the fire not all of the bones would have been destroyed, yet no human bones had been found – despite extensive searches – only bird bones.

Temee and Toi Toi were considered next, with Fraenkel pointing out the inconsistencies in their statements over who had carried the bodies and the body parts. Fraenkel questioned why the police had not required these witnesses to point out where the fire had been or where the fliers had first been encountered. Even though Captain Langley had said this could not have been done at the time due to the heavy rains, Fraenkel wanted to know why it had not been done since.

He even suggested the fact that Rekisang and Morobe would have found it an easy matter to follow any spoor to the fire and that this proved very little.

Fraenkel next questioned why only two witnesses claimed to have seen the fat taken from the bodies melted down, finding the prosecution suggestion that several of the camp were attending to the donkeys flawed. Fraenkel also wanted to know why there were such discrepancies in the description of the airmen's clothes, with some witnesses talking of shirts and vests, and others of shirts and jackets. Fraenkel claimed that these inconsistencies were so large that it could not just be a matter of language and translation. The lack of blood was another point that troubled Fraenkel, asking why many witnesses had not described blood on the airmen's clothing despite their violent deaths and dismemberment. The fact that some witnesses said the fliers' shoes had been removed before their deaths, while others said it was afterwards, was another cause for concern.

According to Fraenkel, the bullet that had been recovered could not definitely be matched to either rifle and that the bullet the police recovered was not from where Twai Twai's shelter had been at the time of the alleged shooting.

Perhaps strangely, Fraenkel then tried to argue that even if two fliers had been found they might not have been Adamson and Edwards. This unlikely idea was based on the fact that the court had not heard any evidence that there were no other Europeans missing at the time.

The items missing from the aeroplane were next on Fraenkel's list, suggesting that the airmen would not have disposed of the Very pistol or the compass, and yet these were never seen by any of the prosecution witnesses. The defence lawyer then claimed that the descriptions of both the water container and the parachute case given in the trial were so divergent that they could be dismissed.

The defence then turned to the evidence of the accused. According to Fraenkel, Twai Twai was clear, concise and superior to the prosecution witnesses, based on the fact he was in the witness box for only a short time. He also claimed that the aeroplane had not been discovered until the end of October, a suggestion that would explain why Twai Twai could not find any spoor around the aircraft.

Keree's statement was dealt with by Fraenkel claiming that it could only have been written by 'no one less than a lunatic' as 'no native of this type would make references' to Tshekedi Khama like that 'unless he was totally mad'.

Before making his final summary, Fraenkel touched on the alternative explanation for the jars of fat offered by his own witnesses. And as noon approached on the sixth day of the trial he concluded:

> My submission is that as far as Twai Twai and Tammai are concerned there is insufficient evidence to connect them with the killing of anybody; and secondly, if there is evidence of a killing there is insufficient evidence to find that those killed were Adamson and Edwards. In the circumstances, we have a very deep hope that they may still be alive. With regard to Keree, the court has heard evidence indicating how far he has been implicated in the crime. His position is no worse than that of the other five accused whom my friend Mr Kelly has adequately dealt with, and with whose remarks I associate myself.
>
> As this is a charge of murder, for which there is only one penalty in the territory, and that is the extreme penalty, so even if there is some sort of proof and the proof is not free from reasonable doubt (in fact I would submit there is a very grave doubt), I submit your lordship will give the accused the benefit of that doubt.

His Lordship, Justice de Beer, then promised that 'the court will take time to consider the verdict', ending proceedings for that week.

JUDGEMENT

With assistance and input from the two District Commissioners and the native assessor, Judge de Beer spent the whole of the Sunday going through the main points of the case. Although today this might have been considered rather hasty, the court was reassembled on the Monday morning to hear the verdict.

The male accused were led into the tin-roofed courthouse for the last time and were soon followed by the five women. The women, only one of whom was out of her teens, once again supported each other by putting their arms over one another's shoulders. Even Keree was described as looking attentive, a change from his usual other-worldliness.

The judge began by reviewing the prosecution case in detail from the moment Airspeed Oxford HN607 left the ground at Kumalo. Oddly, he gave the ranks of the deceased as corporal and second class airmen, despite the RAF witnesses describing them both as sergeants.

Once he had finished describing the activities leading up to the discovery of the missing aircraft, the judge turned to one of the areas that had given him concern during the trial:

> The accused and all the more important witnesses spoke a language with which the members of the court are not acquainted, and in weighing the credibility of the statements made by the different witnesses, we were to a great extent deprived of the advantage of applying what is known as the demeanour test – the gestures of the men in the box, the inflexion of their voices, and the other matters that are included in this undefinable expression 'demeanour'. We are therefore constrained to attach more importance to inconsistencies and contradictions than otherwise would have been the case.

His Lordship went on to say in such cases one must bear in mind the fallibility of human memory, the imperfection of powers of observation, and in the case of the Basarwa, the inability to express in an accurate manner what they might have seen.

Having dealt with the prosecution case, de Beer then looked at the defence. He pointed out that their testimony was one of mere denial – denial of seeing footprints, denial of seeing the airmen, denial of murdering the two white men. Given this, the judge said, it became incumbent upon the court to consider the various contradictions, discrepancies and inconsistencies, and to explain them sufficiently in order to justify a prosecution.

The first of these inconsistencies covered was the headgear the pilots were described as wearing. The fact the prosecution witness had described peaked caps, which bore no resemblance to the leather flying helmets the pilots took off in, even allowing for 'imperfect observation, the fallible memories and the lack of adequate expression of the witnesses', was a matter of 'grave concern' said de Beer. This concern was magnified as the airmen had allegedly been in the company of the Bushmen for many hours. The description of Edwards having dark hair was one that all the prosecution witnesses got wrong, stated the judge, quoting Flight Lieutenant Payne. It was unfortunate that no photos of the missing pilots were available to the judge or even their service records, which would have shown that Gordon Edwards did indeed have brown hair made much darker by his hair cream.

Contradictions over shorts, shoes, which man was killed by the axe, blood on the tunics, and where the property was shared out were all briefly mentioned by the judge before he concentrated on the missing water container. Here, the descriptions given by the Crown witnesses of something they must have prized, given where they lived, differed so much from the actual object missing from the aircraft that the judge concluded that it was likely that some of the witnesses had committed perjury. He went on that this raised the 'more sinister question whether the witnesses were prompted to say they had seen the container'. Captain Langley and Sergeant Preston-Whyte were above suspicion, de Beer claimed, but he reminded the court that there were 'three large parties, one a small commando' looking for the airmen and some of these knew what items were missing from the aircraft.

The judge felt that the question raised above was to be asked in more depth when it came to the story of the parachute container. He was unwilling to believe the descriptions given to the court, as they all underestimated the amount of material in a parachute, which was 74 feet in diameter, by an order of magnitude. If any of the articles from the plane, any possessions, or any signs of the bodies had been found then these inconsistencies may have been overlooked. However, de Beer went on, if five prosecution witnesses had committed perjury on those matters, it was impossible to believe them beyond reasonable doubt on the rest of their testimony, especially when it was not corroborated by any concrete or factual proof. The final part of his judgement is reproduced in full below:

> The administrative officers acting with me in this case, men of experience in these parts, and I have devoted considerable attention of the court to the whole case. There is present with us all an instinctive conviction that certain of the accused were guilty of the dastardly crime. But applying all those tests known to forensic science, applying them to the best of our ability, we have come to the conclusion that there exists a doubt, a very grave doubt in this case, and that we would not be entitled to convict the accused.
>
> The remarks I have made up to this stage are of special application to Twai Twai and Tammai. Keree is in the position that had the Crown evidence been accepted he would have been an accessory after the fact, and this applies also to the women charged, though in their case it would have been to a lesser degree.

But as the case, in our opinion, falls away against the actual two murderers there can be no accessory after the fact when they are charged jointly and in the same indictment.

The verdict of the Court is, therefore, that you are all found not guilty and discharged.

With that the court sprang to life. The Basarwa quietly celebrated, the men shaking hands and chatting excitedly while the women hugged each other and shed a tear or two. The reporters rushed off to get their copy away to their waiting editors, no doubt relieved that they would be returning to South Africa the following day. Among the public who had followed the trial there was mute disappointment, with many feeling that justice had not been done. Certainly they were not the only ones to be uneasy with the outcome, and the ripples the not guilty verdict would cause would travel far and have many unexpected consequences.

5

AFTERMATH

THE ROYAL AIR FORCE

Even before the verdict, the alleged crime had affected life in the Rhodesian Air Training Group. Within a month of the missing aeroplane being found, the officer commanding the training scheme, Air Vice Marshal Meredith, had received a letter from the Resident Commissioner of Bechuanaland telling him that it was thought the pilots had been murdered.

The letter informed the RAF officer that the Bushmen in the area where the plane landed were considered 'bad people' by the natives and that this particular family had been implicated in a previous double murder of two Europeans. It mentioned that Tshekedi Khama had been very helpful in the search and investigation and that there were high hopes of justice being done, although it warned that this would take time. The Resident Commissioner suggested that airmen be issued with rifles and more up-to-date maps, something the Commissioner was willing to help with. The rifles would be useful protection from wild animals as well as Bushmen and of course could be used to gain food for any downed airman. The letter ended by saying that the vast majority of natives, including Bushmen, were friendly, and it was very unfortunate that Edwards and Adamson had just been in the wrong place at the wrong time.

The RAF took this advice and soon ordered that all pilots should be armed when flying, usually with 0.303 rifles backed up by side arms. This was already in place by the time the trial started. Alf Eves, the instructor, added an additional Colt 0.45 to his personal armoury on subsequent flights. Another change to the training syllabus was a greater emphasis on survival training, including much more useful advice for coping with a forced landing in the bush, as well as the more usual escape techniques that would be of use in the European theatre of operations. Interestingly, there was no discussion of introducing of an African 'goolie chit'. The infamous goolie chit had long been carried by aircrew flying in areas where the 'natives' were not entirely trusted to be friendly, especially in the Middle East and Afghanistan. These one-sided letters would include a short message printed in the local languages requesting that the pilot be returned, sometimes in return for a reward, with all his parts still attached. They also included a short collection of useful advice and phrases for the downed crew.

The criminal trial had made little headway into why the two pilots had become so lost and the RAF could not find a conclusive answer either. One suggestion was that the compass was faulty in some way, but this did not explain how the pilots had got as far as the final waypoint, as proved by the photo they had taken. The favoured explanation was that on the last turn the pilots had misread their compass, placing 'red on black' and flying a reciprocal course for some time before realising their mistake. This idea was corroborated to some extent by the fact that the plane had been flying in the rough direction of Bulawayo when the Basarwa hunting party first saw it, suggesting the pilots had realised their mistake.

Roy Nesbit, a Senior Navigation Officer at one of the Service Flying Training Schools in Rhodesia at the time of the disappearance, came up with a simple solution to what was a common error. His suggestion of taping over the southern end of the compass grid was adopted by the RAF, earning him a £10 'inventor's award'. Within a year a new type of compass with a T-shaped grid was introduced, eliminating further mistakes. Although it may have been little consolation for the families involved, the loss of Adamson and Edwards did improve aviation safety.

However, for those not directly involved in the case, life went on much as before. Despite the extensive press coverage, within six months of the trial the story had achieved something of a mythical status. The constant turnover of instructors and trainee pilots in Rhodesia meant that those with personal knowledge of the case were soon dispersed around the world. Those who had trained with Walter and Gordon had finished their course within a month of the pair's disappearance and had been posted to operational units, many with Bomber Command. Harry Tait, who had been with Gordon and Walter since the journey from Egypt, was posted to George in South Africa for further training before being sent to fly Martin Marauders in the Middle East. His mother was in the habit of sending newspaper cuttings along with her letters and it was in Sardinia that the news of what had happened to his friends eventually reached him. For those who arrived in Rhodesia after the trial, Adamson and Edwards were just another pair of prospective pilots who had not survived training.

Over time the details of the case became more muddled in the collective memory. The missing Oxford became a Tiger Moth, a Harvard, or even a Dakota. The Bushmen remained a constant part of the story and while the giraffe hunting was often mentioned, the motive for the killing became more imaginative as the story became little more than a game of Chinese whispers. One version had the Bushmen believing that the pilots were government spies that had been sent to ensure that the Basarwa received punishment for their various crimes. Another told that the Bushmen had never seen an aeroplane before and that they believed the pilots to be gods and that by eating the white men they would receive their heavenly powers.

'A STRIKING EXAMPLE
OF BRITISH JUSTICE'

The press reaction to the verdict was one of surprise, but on the whole the coverage was fair and balanced. The main exception was the *New Rhodesian* which expressed outrage at the outcome of the trial, perhaps pandering to the racial ideas that its readers held. This, combined with police fears about retribution towards the prosecution witnesses, meant that there was considerable pressure on the Bechuanaland authorities to be seen to be doing something.

Forsyth-Thompson, the Resident Commissioner, took immediate legal advice, ironically from Kelly, the second defence advocate. Forsyth had received information from the police in Francistown that Twai Twai's brother, Letsami, had threatened revenge on those who had given evidence in the case and Forsyth was desperately trying to come up with some way to delay the return of Twai Twai and Tammai to Nata. His initial plan was to have the pair charged with not paying Hut Tax, but, as many other Basarwa did not pay either, a conviction was by no means certain. However, given the evidence submitted by both sides in the trial, it seemed that a charge of illegal hunting would be incontestable. Kelly considered that this would be legal, but that charging someone with a minor crime connected with a major one that they had been acquitted of was 'very bad form'.

Twai Twai and Tammai were therefore arrested in Francistown on their way back to Nata, charged and sentenced to three months hard labour. Ellenberger, the District Commissioner who had sat in the trial, confirmed this in a letter to Forsyth-Thompson on 18 October 1944. He also mentioned that their guns had been confiscated and he also revealed his unrelated concerns that the rains had not arrived yet.

A week before this letter had been sent, Forsyth-Thompson had called an emergency meeting with Tshekedi Khama to discuss possible solutions to the matter. Even before the trial, the Resident Commissioner had considered the idea of relocating the Bushmen. This was first suggested to the DC at Kasane, in the far north, close to Victoria Falls, who claimed they would 'be very difficult' to control and that he had enough problems with crime and marijuana smoking among his own natives. Present at the meeting were the Resident Commissioner, his deputy, Captain Potts, and Mackenzie on the British side, while on the native side there were Chief Khama, three of the chief's headmen, and Seitshiro Moshweu. Mackenzie and Moshweu had both sat as officials during the case.

Tshilwane, one of the Bangwato headmen, opened the meeting by telling of the threats Twai Twai's brother had been making. He then said what he thought of the Basarwa. 'They are difficult to control; animals are easier. Animals go in herds, Masarwa live in small groups. They never live in a community together.' He was in favour of relocating the Basarwa and putting them under Bangwato control. If this worked, it would be a lesson to others. He claimed that they had tried with Twai Twai before, giving him cattle which he had tended for a while before leaving the cows in a kraal and reverting to hunting. The headman finished by saying that travellers were scared to go through the lands near Twai Twai and that the whole Molele family should be collected.

Moshweu, who had been the native assessor in the trial, then told of investigating Twai Twai's father after the death of a trader. This was in 1896, but it was two years before the victim's bones were found. He said the Molele family were constantly in trouble, but that it had always proved impossible to collect evidence against them.

The next two headmen both said that the Basarwa were too wild to control and that they would murder anybody that tried. Forsyth-Thompson disagreed, saying it was possible for them to learn new customs and to be controlled. He backed his argument up by pointing out that some Basarwa were already domesticated, earning a living by growing crops.

Tshekedi was the next to speak, and he did so in a much more measured way than his fellow tribesmen. He started by describing the Twai Twai family tree in detail. Twai Twai's father had had at least two wives, and the children from the first marriage had been well behaved. Indeed, one of them had worked for the British South African Police, tracking down fugitives who had fled Rhodesia to take refuge in the Bechuanaland Protectorate. From the second marriage it was clear that Twai Twai was the black sheep, having been accused of being involved in the death of a husband to a woman he wanted to marry himself. Yet one of Twai Twai's many sons, Chimi, had approached Khama to herd his cattle and Tshekedi said he had done this well, with his branch of the family causing no trouble. This could not be said of Tammai and Twai Twai, who abandoned their cattle every time they went hunting.

The chief then made some suggestions as to the way forward. He doubted that the Basarwa could be collected peacefully, given the previous animosity between his people and the Bushmen. Tshekedi was also against the idea of constant police patrols, as he thought this would further alienate the Basarwa from authority. Instead, he suggested that the government set up cattle posts and allow the Basarwa to gravitate towards them. This would provide employment and introduce the Bushmen to civilisation. Khama thought that a ban on hunting would not be enforceable, although forbidding the hunting of giraffe might be. However, he thought the murder of the airmen justified the disarmament of the Bushmen in general.

While he thought the relocation of the Basarwa was impractical, Tshekedi said that he favoured moving the Molele family to his reserve where they could be observed and kept away from trouble.

The Resident Commissioner was obviously pleased with this response as it matched Forsyth-Thompson's own plans. He closed the meeting by agreeing a four-step plan. First, the Molele family would be removed to a cattle post near Serowe, the capital of the Bangwato reserve. Second, the government would establish two or three cattle posts or farms to the north of Nata. Third, all the Basarwa in the region would be disarmed, and, finally, a permanent police post at Nata would be established.

Forsyth-Thompson lost little time in forwarding these plans to the High Commissioner in South Africa. In this letter he mentioned the allegations of previous murders and the fact that the not guilty verdict had raised Twai Twai's reputation as a witchdoctor, as many now thought he was immune from punishment. The only change to the four earlier points was that the new cattle posts were now to be known as 'Livestock Improvement Centres' and were to be of a more educational nature.

After receiving this information, Huggard, who should have been the judge at the trial but who was still standing in for the High Commissioner in Pretoria, forwarded to London his own proposal for collective punishment of the Basarwa in the form of a punitive raid. Along with this idea, Huggard also forwarded all the local press clippings on the case.

It was the beginning of November by the time a copy of this missive reached Forsyth-Thompson in Mafeking and he reacted with some alarm to the idea of any kind of raid. He wrote back to Huggard stating that opening a police post in Nata was sufficient in combination with the banishment of the Molele family, who were at the root of most of the problems. He included a draft removal order with the letter. He said that his plan to remove any unregistered weapons from the Bushmen would be implemented over two years as not to cause hardship and that his ultimate aim was to have the Basarwa tilling the land. In addition, the budget of £300 per annum for the police station in Nata was included, along with more detail of how the post would operate. The plan was to have five policemen, including a European NCO, two messengers and several camels. The camels were to be brought from the police breeding station that had been set up in Tsabong in the south as they were felt to be better suited than horses to the harsh conditions at Nata. WNLA were offering temporary accommodation so the post could open quickly.

London then offered their view, with the Dominions Office also alarmed by the suggestion of any sort of raid against the Bushmen. They also expressed concern about the disarmament of the Basarwa, on the grounds that they could face increased danger from wild animals. In no uncertain terms, they let Huggard know that the verdict in the trial should be considered 'a striking example of British justice and it would be a pity to spoil the good effect by any action that might be represented as resembling, though in a very minor degree, Nazi methods of dealing with subject peoples'. The communication's last offering was that the Dominions Office trusted the newly arrived permanent High Commissioner, Sir Evelyn Baring, would be able to deal with the matter satisfactorily.

This led to a flurry of telegrams over the next few days between Forsyth-Thompson in Mafeking, the newly arrived Baring in Pretoria, and the Dominions Office in London. The outcome of these was that Forsyth-Thompson's four-point plan was given the go ahead. However, the Secretary of State in London wanted to ensure that the plan did not give the appearance of 'letting loose' Tshekedi's people on the Basarwa, especially given the Bangwato's historical treatment of Bushmen as 'serfs'.

In the meantime, Forsyth-Thompson had prepared extended notes on the case that he added to the transcript of the court proceedings. These were forwarded to Pretoria, London and also to the RAF in Rhodesia. In this four-page essay, the Resident Commissioner disagreed with the reasoning of the judge that the Crown witnesses had committed perjury. He admitted there was some doubt in the case, but was of the opinion that the discrepancies in the testimony of the key witnesses were nothing more than you would expect from 'primitive people, testifying to what they had observed and heard a year previously'. Forsyth-Thompson claimed that the prosecution had spread its net too wide and, with hindsight, it would have been better just to charge Twai Twai and Tammai. All the women had given statements implicating the two men in the murder, but these statements could only be used against themselves and not as evidence against Twai Twai or Tammai. If these witnesses, and possibly Keree, had been used as prosecution witnesses, a conviction of the ringleaders would have been much more likely.

By the end of November, the notice banning ownership of ammunition and guns by Basarwa on Crown lands had been proclaimed. In a typical piece of civil service pedantry, there was a long discussion over whether muzzle loaders qualified as guns, but eventually common sense prevailed and they were. Despite his plans going ahead, Forsyth-Thompson still felt under pressure. The main source of this was *The New Rhodesian*, a right-wing newspaper in favour of whites-only rule, that was blaming the acquittal of the Bushmen on weak governance of Bechuanaland. The Resident Commissioner asked Baring for permission to inform the press of what action the government was proposing, but the High Commissioner refused, saying that it would be better to offer a press release after the plans had borne fruit.

On 21 December the District Commissioner at Francistown travelled to Nata with Tshekedi Khama to explain these plans to the Basarwa. With him travelled Preston-Whyte as Captain Langley was ill. The next day they spoke with a group of seventy Bushmen where the Commissioner told the congregation what was going to happen and about the new police post. Those present on the banishment list were served with their notices and told arrangements would be made for transport the following day. There was a noticeable lack of comment or remonstration at this. The day after this meeting saw a lorry containing a handful of Bushmen arrive in Francistown, where the District Commissioner oversaw the release of Twai Twai and Tammai. After informing them of their

To:

DAMUU: Wife of TWAI TWAI MOLELE.

I am instructed by His Excellency the High Commissioner in terms of section three of Proclamation No. 15 of 1907 under High Commissioner's telegram No. 128 of 22nd November, 1944, to direct you to confine yourself during His Majesty's pleasure within such limits of the Bechuanaland Protectorate as lie south of the 22nd degree of Latitude and west of the 27th degree of Longitude.

RESIDENT COMMISSIONER.

Resident Commissioner's Office,

Mafeking.

11th January, 1945.

I certify that I have this day, at Bojananene served a copy of this banishment order on the within named DAMUU wife of TWAI TWAI and at the same time explained to her the nature thereof.

ASSISTANT DISTRICT COMMISSIONER.

16 February 1946

Dambe's (misspelled here) banishment order. (*Botswana National Archives*)

disarmament and banishment they were placed in a second truck and, accompanied by the DC and Tshekedi, the small convoy set off for Serowe. On the way, the Commissioner's truck broke down, but Tshekedi fared even worse as his truck ended up on its side. Reinforcements came in the form of a WNLA vehicle, a lorry hired from the local Joubert family, and a commandeered Tsetse fly truck.

The new year saw the resettled Basarwa living off bags of grain in Shashane, just outside Tshekedi's capital. Tshekedi had promised to organise compensation for the cattle the family group had left behind in Nata. However, trouble was never far away from the Molele family and three weeks into 1945 news reached Mafeking that Letsami, Twai Twai's brother, had murdered his estranged wife. Letsami apparently claimed that, following Twai Twai's acquittal, he was safe from prosecution.

By the end of March there were thirty-two Basarwa living in Shashane. They were still waiting for their livestock or compensation from Tshekedi, who was promising that he had the matter under control. In the meantime he was supplying bags of grain for the Bushmen to eat. Despite these problems, it was considered that they had settled well and had caused no further concerns. The police post at Nata was up and running, with camel patrols into the bush underway. Several Martini Henry rifles had been handed in, along with many muzzle loaders, and these were to be auctioned off or destroyed in Francistown. However, the disarming of the Basarwa was still continuing on a gradual basis. Letsami had been arrested and charged with his wife's murder. All of this news, along with mention of how helpful and cooperative Tshekedi had been throughout, was forwarded to London. London sent back an acknowledgement that they now considered the file closed.

TALIFANG

Talifang, one of the defence witnesses, was among those transported to Shashane, but for her the case was not completely over.

She was married to the WNLA camp manager at Nonga and he was well respected by the camp management. His relentless pressuring of his boss whenever he visited Nata eventually led the District Manager of WNLA to write to the Resident Commissioner in Mafeking, pleading for her release.

This request was considered by Forsyth-Thompson and, while it took some time, he acquiesced and Talifang returned to her beloved Mosweu. His decision may have been influenced by the good reports he had received on the progress of the relocated Basarwa. They were still under the stewardship of Tshekedi, but many were now living near Phikwe and had been helping Khama's men hunt leopards over the winter.

Talefang's release coincided with the issue of the final banishment order, and by the middle of 1946, the Resident Commissioner's office considered the matter closed.

THE EDWARDS FAMILY

Muriel, Gordon Edwards' sister, had become suspicious when there was a break in Gordon's correspondence. At first she had put this down to a simple problem with the post, as she knew her brother was very conscientious when it came to his family. On his last leave before going to Africa he had promised to bring back a doll for Muriel's daughter, Rosalind. However, when she saw the story of the Francistown hearing in one of the national papers, she had her first clue as to what had happened to her brother.

Her first attempt to confirm her suspicions by contacting the newspaper's editor ended in failure when he told her that he could not release further details. She did not give up and while the paper could supply few further details, they did eventually confirm that Gordon was one of the pilots concerned. She then confronted her mother who admitted that it was true.

Sarah Edwards was devastated by the loss of the son she was so devoted to, and, despite her strong personality, she found it impossible to cope with Gordon's death. Her only solution was to obliterate all evidence of Gordon's existence and to effectively write him out of history. She avoided talking about him and threw away anything that reminded her of him. To avoid discussion with neighbours the family was again upended, this time to Pontyclun. This led to Gordon's name appearing on both villages' war memorials, as well as on a commemorative plaque at Miskin Hall Cricket Club's new pavilion.

Gordon's father did return to the region from Scotland – perhaps Gordon's death had something to do with this. Despite not having gained a divorce from Sarah, Mr Edwards set up home in a neighbouring village with a lady, who he passed off as 'Mrs Edwards'.

He became involved in local politics and achieved reasonable success. Poignantly, one of his duties was to lay a wreath on Remembrance Sunday at the war memorial in Miskin that included his son's name.

Muriel was to bear the brunt of her mother's pain, with Sarah Edwards making no secret of the fact that she wished that Gordon was still alive and that she would have been happier if Muriel had been the one that had been killed.

Over time the two women became reconciled, even though they never became really close. Sarah did, however, help look after the growing Rosalind. Rosalind was usually a good child, but when she did misbehave she could certainly outrun the increasingly wide Sarah. Rosalind remembers attending a political meeting in the late 1940s where her grandfather and his new lady friend were introduced as 'Mr and Mrs Edwards'. Rosalind stood up with childish innocence and informed the hall 'that is not the real Mrs Edwards!'

Sarah never had another relationship, with no man being able to live up to her image of Gordon. Nor mentally did she fully recover. As she grew older she moved in with her daughter before developing signs of dementia. The final straw for Muriel was when her mother locked several people in the local post office. Sarah Edwards died in a home for the elderly in the late 1970s, still mourning her son.

'THE TEN THOUSAND MEN'

With the war over, the Batswana volunteers spread around a wide arc of the Mediterranean had looked forward to a speedy return to the empty spaces of Botswana. However, prisoners of war from the Far East were given priority in terms of shipping. This was understandable as there were around 70,000 British, Commonwealth and Dutch prisoners, many of whom had been in captivity for four years since the fall of Singapore. The Japanese had developed a horrific reputation for their treatment of their detainees. Beatings, torture, forced labour, starvation rations, along with poor medical treatment, had led to the death of more than a quarter of the European prisoners they had taken. The survivors were, in the vast majority of cases, in dire need of speedy evacuation and medical care.

This meant that some of the Bechuanaland troops had to wait until the first quarter of 1946 before they could be shipped back to South Africa. For a handful of companies in Palestine this proved too much and they refused to dismiss from morning parade. This non-violent protest lasted only a couple of days.

Any negative feelings disappeared once on board the ships until Durban and the sound of marching songs reverberated around the hulls of the transports. Forsyth-Thompson was on hand in Durban to welcome the first troops home. Once disembarked, they went to Clairewood camp, where nearly four years earlier Gordon Edwards and Walter Adamson had stayed. Here they were formally demobilised, but some of them faced a further delay with a shortage of trains to make the journey back to the protectorate. However, each man received fitted civilian clothes, including a suit, hat, shirt, tie, socks and shoes, a testimonial and a £10 gratuity.

A handful of Batswana had a final duty to attend to however, with a selection of sergeants and sergeant-majors being chosen to represent the High Commission Territories at the Victory Parade in London in front of King George. Others paraded in Durban, but the parade that meant the most to the majority of the returning soldiers was the one held in front of their tribes and chiefs. The Resident Commissioner represented the British Government at each of these.

One year later there was a great reunion in Lobatsi, with uniformed black troops coming from all parts of Bechuanaland to receive thanks from the King in person. The white royal train stood in a siding in the small town where the fate of the murderers of Gordon Edwards and Walter Adamson had been decided. Surrounded by the green April hills, King George, his wife, and two young princesses witnessed the final parade of the 'ten thousand men'.

During the course of the conflict thirty-two Batswana had been mentioned in dispatches, earning a deserved reputation for efficiency and professionalism for the whole Bechuanaland group. Chitu Bakombi and Rasebolai Kgamane were both awarded the British Empire Medal while Regimental Sergeant Major Molwa Sekgoma earned an MBE, then a very rare distinction for a Motswana.

Two hundred and ten men never returned home and another five hundred and sixty had brought back wounds serious enough to qualify them for disability pensions.

After the excitement of war, culminating with the royal visit of thanks, Bechuanaland returned to its normal state of sleepy happiness. Some of those who had seen the world during their service brought back some political ideas, but, for the most part, soldiers went back to the cattle posts and the fields, tending the maize while the world slowly forgot about them.

POSTSCRIPT

TSHEKEDI KHAMA'S DOWNFALL AND SERETSE'S RISE

Tshekedi Khama had earned the gratitude of the British administration for not only the handling of the 'Bushmen Case', but also for his support for the war effort. The Bangwato supplied more men and raised more funds than any of the other Batswana tribes. His battles of the 1930s and his temporary suspension by Rey now seemed a long way away. However, given his strong personality, this good relationship with the administration could not last. The cause of his next fall from grace came from an unexpected quarter.

At the end of the war Tshekedi and the Bangwato sent their future chief, Seretse Khama, to study in England. After completing his degree at Fort Hare in 1944 he spent a year at Oxford before joining the Inner Temple to become a barrister. It was here that he met Ruth Williams, a white middle-class girl from Blackheath. After a whirlwind romance, Seretse informed his uncle that he intended to marry Ruth. Tshekedi was vehemently against the union as it went against Tswana tradition and he was joined in his opposition by the British administration. A mixed marriage in the 1940s was controversial enough, but when it involved potentially one of the most important chiefs of a black African colony surrounded by racially obsessed white-ruled countries it was too much for the British Government.

Despite the opposition, Ruth and Seretse married. The ceremony was a civil one as political pressure had caused the Bishop of London to cancel a church service. Seretse returned to Serowe to explain his case to the Bangwato and after two difficult Kgotla meetings, where he threatened to abdicate, he won over the majority of the tribe. Tshekedi continued to oppose the marriage and took some of his supporters to live with the neighbouring

Bakwena. Many suspected that the old man did not want to give up the chieftainship to his nephew. The British, under pressure from Rhodesia and South Africa, ordered a report into Seretse's conduct and suitability for becoming *kgosi* (chief). When Sir Walter Harrigin reported that Seretse was indeed 'a fit and proper person', his report was buried in the finest traditions of the British Civil Service. Instead, Seretse was invited to England for talks on his accession. Once in London the government tried to offer Seretse money and jobs, including the ambassadorship to Jamaica, in return for giving up the chieftainship. When he refused he was banished from Botswana for five years and forced to remain in the United Kingdom. At the same time Tshekedi was banished from the Bangwato reserve. During this difficult time, Seretse was represented by Percy Fraenkel, the lawyer who had successfully defended Twai Twai Molele.

The Bangwato refused to elect a new chief and Seretse's popularity only grew with his mistreatment by the British. Protests, tax avoidance and even violent riots ensued. Seretse also had his supporters in Parliament, Fenner Brockway organising the Council for Defence of Seretse. The fact that South Africa was becoming increasingly racist and anti-British meant that it was becoming less likely that Bechuanaland could be incorporated into the Union. Independence for all of Britain's African territories was on the cards, although there was a concern in the protectorate's case because of the number of different tribes that inhabited the land. Eventually, Tshekedi travelled to Britain in 1956 to bury the hatchet and Seretse was allowed to travel home, but only as a private citizen and not as a chief. This mattered little to the thousands that turned up to welcome him on his return. Tshekedi once again was back in favour, but this was to be his final recovery as he died in 1959.

Seretse Khama never lost his popularity and it was no surprise that his Botswana Democratic Party won the first elections in the protectorate. His personality was influential in drawing all the Batswana

The statue of Sir Seretse Khama that stands outside of Parliament.

tribes together to form a united country. When the Union Jack was drawn down under unusual September rains to be replaced by the blue, white and black of the new Botswana flag, it was Seretse Khama who took control of what was still one of the poorest countries in the world. The following year, 1967, one of the world's biggest deposits of diamonds was found at Orapa. Later this would be joined by another mine at Jwaneng, giving Botswana the planet's biggest diamond mines in terms of both volume and value. Negotiating a very good deal with de Beers, Botswana went on to become arguably the most successful African country. Seretse Khama would win two more elections and would be knighted by the British before his untimely death from cancer in 1980. Ruth lived for another twenty-two years, earning a warm respect as the 'first lady' of the country.

Despite being surrounded by political chaos in neighbouring states as white rule was violently challenged and eventually overcome, Botswana maintained its status as a peaceful, multi-party democracy. Indeed, faced by the situation in South Africa, the new country went out of its way to show that it was race blind. Its capital, the newly built city of Gaborone, was for many years the world's fastest growing city. The diamond wealth, unlike the mineral money in many African countries, was invested in infrastructure, health and education.

Today, Botswana is undoubtedly one of Africa's success stories. Although rural poverty and HIV/AIDS have provided large challenges, the country continues to develop at breakneck speed. New malls and even 'skyscrapers' are going up in Gaborone on what seems like a monthly basis, yet the country has maintained its friendly small village feel. One feels that both Charles Rey and Tshekedi Khama would have been impressed.

IMPACT ON THE BUSHMEN

During a war where more than 20 million soldiers lost their lives in the biggest conflict history had ever seen, it was perhaps unexpected that the murder of Adamson and Edwards would capture the world's attention in the way that it did. Equally surprising in many ways was that the British Government spent so much time and effort trying to convict a family group of hunters from the edge of the Kalahari in the middle of the Second World War. However, the prosecution of Twai Twai Molele was to have significant effects on the future of the Bechuanaland Protectorate's Bushmen.

As well as the police station in Nata, the administration set up game camps at Modala and Sepako in order to crack down on illegal poaching of the type Twai Twai had been involved in. Tshekedi Khama was asked to help in the relocation of the remaining 'wild' Bushmen in the Nata region. This was done by using mounted patrols to round up the Tyua and ensure that the disarming orders had been carried out. Those captured in these sweeps were resettled in villages to the south of the Nata River. Here they were used to carry out work in the fields or as cattle herders, the same fate as many of their ancestors. The resettlement efforts led to conflict between the Tyua and the Bangwato, with persistent rumours of Bushmen being beaten and even killed during the process. Many Tyua drifted farther south to work for other tribes rather than stay with the Bangwato.

The government did keep its promise to establish a Livestock Improvement Centre near Pandamatenga, about 130 miles north of Nata. Here work was found for some Tyua, initially in the construction of fences and then as cattle herders. For the first time Bushmen were paid for the services in cash and not just milk, but this also brought social problems to the Tyua as some people grew richer than others, which had not occurred before. Unfortunately, a combination of poisonous plants and losses to lions and hyenas led to low productivity and the cattle centre was closed in the mid-1950s. The Tyua employed there had tried their best to protect the herds from predators, with at least two of their number being killed on lion hunts. One of those who lost their lives was one of Twai Twai Molele's sons.

Despite this, the Tyua in Bechuanaland probably fared better than their compatriots on the Rhodesian side of the border. Having been forced out of many areas by white farmers or by the creation of game parks they often found life difficult with their Kalanga or Ndebele neighbours, who viewed them with suspicion and often accused them of stealing cattle. After Ian Smith's Unilateral Declaration of Independence many Tyua men found themselves induced into fighting, either for the government or the liberation forces. Many families were resettled in 'protected villages' with heavy restriction on weapons and hunting, further disrupting traditional life. Even after Zimbabwe gained independence the Tyua benefitted little, largely being ignored, even to the extent that at one point a government official claimed that Zimbabwe had no Bushmen.

In independent Botswana the events in Nata were gradually forgotten by those who had heard of them; the vast majority of the population had not. The introduction of universal primary education, the building of village clinics and the provision of clean running water meant that by the mid-1980s life was changing for the Tyua and other groups that had access to the new infrastructure.

The problem was that the new roads and facilities were concentrated down the eastern side of the country, largely following the development that Rhodes' railway had brought. Those San Bushmen in the central Kalahari or near Ghanzi saw little benefit. The government of Botswana decided to build new villages with clinics and schools and relocate people there. This met with much opposition from those Bushmen who did not want to give up their ancestral lands. In the 1990s there were forced relocations of San from the Central Kalahari Game Reserve (CKGR) for game conservation within the massive park. While many accepted that the relocations started with the best of intentions, many families struggled to cope with the change in lifestyle. Most of the new villages were still too far from the developing east of the country to offer any long-term job prospects and alcohol dependence became a major problem. Later relocations from the CKGR were tainted by the suspicion that the area might contain diamond deposits.

The process of relocation has led to several High Court cases in Botswana that have generally found in favour of the Bushmen. Diamond mining has already begun. The handling of this issue is perhaps the one black mark against an otherwise very happy and successful country. Today a couple of hundred Bushmen still live relatively traditional hunter-gatherer lifestyles, while the vast majority with San roots are integrated, with mixed success, into Botswana's developing society.

TWAI TWAI

Twai Twai Molele went on to live a long life, eventually drifting back to the Nata region. It became commonly accepted that the story portrayed by the prosecution was the correct one and many of those involved acknowledged this was so. Twai Twai is one of those alleged to have admitted his part in the murder of the airmen.

In the mid-1970s he was interviewed by Robert Hitchcock, now a professor and acknowledged expert on indigenous groups, especially in southern Africa. Hitchcock was then a young researcher who had come across the story of Gordon and Walter's murder and appreciated the insight into Tyua life that the trial documents provided. He made copies of Captain Langley's sketch maps, which have since been lost from the court files. These, along with the case notes, gave a glimpse into a way of life that was rapidly disappearing. Hitchcock managed to track down many of those who had been involved in the case, including some of the police who had carried out the investigation. However, when he asked Twai Twai about his version of events the reply was, 'Who is still interested in those things?'

Today Twai Twai is remembered in the *Historical Dictionary of Botswana* as 'a social bandit of Shua descent'.

THE TEN THOUSAND: RRE MOLATLHWE

Some of the troops that had served the Empire so well in its time of need, such as Philip Matante and Amos Dambe, played significant parts in the creation of Botswana. Their experience overseas, especially meeting people from other colonies, gave rise to a new political awareness. This was reflected upon their return in the setting up of the first Setswana newspaper, *Tlou*, which today lives on as the government-produced *Daily News*. The reading of newspapers was a habit many of the soldiers brought back with them.

However, many did just drift back into village life and their stories were quickly forgotten as independence arrived and the freedom struggles in neighbouring countries became the focus of a new generation. War pensions became the sole reminder of their youthful adventures. Unfortunately, they began to feel that they did not get the recognition they deserved, either from the Botswana Government or their former British masters. This began to change in the early part of the new millennium when visiting academics helped the veteran association to collect memories and quickly disappearing oral tales. When this was brought to the attention of the British High Commission they organised an annual dinner for Remembrance Day.

I was fortunate enough to be invited to the 2013 dinner in Kanye, southern Botswana. Hosted by the British High Commissioner and with a British military presence from Pretoria, it was a real honour to meet some of the final survivors of the conflict. The youngest was in his early 90s while the oldest was over 100, yet they all retained a humble feeling of loyalty to Britain and a sense of humour. Interestingly, this was the first celebration to invite the Botswana knitters, the ladies who had learnt how to make the hats and scarves that had made their way to Syrian winters.

The author and Mr Molatlhwe, one of the Ten Thousand.

One veteran was invited to talk to secondary school students at Maru-a-Pula School, where he amazed children not only with his memories but with his physical fitness. Ephraim Molatlhwe had felt a debt of gratitude for the British protection that Queen Victoria had bestowed upon Bechuanaland and had no hesitation in signing up to fight Hitler. He remembers being told of the horrors of what was happening in Germany and especially the treatment of Jewish university staff and the way the education system had been affected in Germany. Given the almost complete lack of any educational system in Bechuanaland at the time, this was a curious argument for recruiters to have used. Like many of his comrades, Molatlhwe spoke no English when he arrived for his training in Lobatsi. Drilling by a very vocal sergeant-major was his introduction to the language of Shakespeare and to this day his English consists largely of stock phrases learnt from the British Army seventy years earlier.

His first train ride was followed by his first sight of the sea at the Durban coast. Molatlhwe heard the explosions of the torpedoes that sent hundreds of his Lesotho colleague to the bottom of the ocean. He had vivid memories of coming under fire for the first time and admitted, in his phrase-book English, that 'I nearly shit myself'. When asked by one of the students what he did when the Germans shot at him, the 93-year-old dived lengthwise, without any hesitation, down to the cold, hard, concrete floor – amusing the children and more than slightly scaring his minder from the British High Commission. To prove that he was still up to the task, he completed ten push-ups before springing back upright.

A few more examples of drill, including his Lee Enfield rifle, concluded with a standing ovation and a quick march to the exit, and this tiny veteran left the children with a new understanding of their history – for many it was the first time they had heard that their great-grandfathers had fought in the war.

A measure of Rre Molatlhwe's humility is that when we were talking to him over tea and scones in the staffroom he was much prouder of the actions of his grandfather. Molatlhwe senior had been captured by a party of Mzilikazi's Zulu warriors yet, with the son of a local chief, had engineered his escape. To this wonderful old soldier, this was a much more exciting story than anything that he had done.

RATG

At the end of the Second World War the Rhodesian Air Training Group continued to operate, but at a much reduced rate. An administrative re-organisation was undertaken at the start of 1946 and a more serious one in December. The latter saw the organisation lose its Group status, being downgraded to the Rhodesian Air Training Wing. The following year saw the re-birth of the Southern Rhodesian Air Force which took over some of the RAF facilities as well as some ex-RAF aircraft. These included Spitfire Mk 22s, which would soon be joined by jet Vampires.

With increased tensions between the old allies and the start of the Cold War, the RAF realised that it would again be short of trained personnel and it was decided to return the Rhodesian operation to full Group status. Although it never reached the numbers it had enjoyed during the war, the mistrust in Europe and its consequences, such as the Korean War, meant that once again African skies were filled with prospective Royal Air Force pilots who would rarely return to the continent once their training was complete. However, this renaissance could not last as the United Kingdom was effectively bankrupt. The British Government was closing down Flying Training Schools in the UK and, despite the benefits of the weather in Rhodesia, it was impossible to justify the RATG's continuing operation. The final RAF 'wings' parade was held at the end of October 1953 and by March the following year the last British personnel and equipment had been shipped home.

Even with the ending of RAF training a close relationship was maintained between the two air forces. The extent of this relationship can be gauged by the fact that single examples of Britain's nuclear deterrent were sometimes deployed to Salisbury. The flights, known as

'Lone Rangers', were used by the RAF to test the ability of its Vulcan and Victor crews to operate self-sufficiently far from home. In 1964, Rhodesia was visited by the third of the V-bombers, the Vickers Valiant, in order to map parts of Rhodesia and Bechuanaland. The three photographic aircraft from 543 Squadron spent eleven weeks mapping an area roughly the size of France, Germany and England combined. Echoing the experiences of the wartime comrades, the crews found Rhodesia to have 'better food, better beer, better weather and friendlier people'. The nightlife was described as 'demanding'. Even with these massive state-of-the-art machines, flights still took off at dawn to avoid the rough air and, even with the latest radar and electronic aids, navigation of the featureless bush was still tricky. In an age of GPS, where accurate navigation is taken for granted, these reconnaissance flights demonstrated the problems Gordon and Walter faced using their old maps. The best example of this was the fact that Kariba Dam's official position was moved by more than three miles following the 1964 survey flights.

Rhodesia's drift away from the United Kingdom's vision of the future for Africa came to a sudden head with Ian Smith's Unilateral Declaration of Independence in 1965. This brought to an end formal links between the two air forces. Indeed, the RAF was soon involved in an operation against its former ally. The British Government erected radio aerials on top of Nyangabgwe Hill in Francistown to transmit propaganda into its rebellious colony and was worried about their vulnerability to ground attack. RAF Argosy transports, including the example preserved at the RAF Museum at Cosford, were used to ferry in the radio equipment and also two companies of Welsh Fusiliers to protect the transmission centre. This caused tension between the pro-Smith whites in Francistown and the local population.

With Botswana gaining independence in 1966, giving hope to those wanting to see majority rule in Rhodesia, tensions were high between the two countries for the next sixteen years. Regular incursions by Rhodesian forces were one of the main reasons behind Botswana's decision to create the Botswana Defence Force in 1977. Soon afterwards, fifteen BDF soldiers were killed by a Rhodesian Army ambush inside Botswana. In 1979 a Botswana Defence Force Defender, a light transport aircraft, was shot down while it was supporting BDF troops reacting to a Rhodesian Special Forces operation near Francistown. Although the Defender managed to make a forced landing at Francistown, it marked the Rhodesian Air Force's last 'kill'. For a country that had done so much to help defeat the evil of Hitler, and whose sacrifices were at that time still remembered in the form of the Vulcans of No. 44 'Rhodesian' Squadron RAF, this was a sad ending. Within three years it would become the Air Force of the Republic of Zimbabwe.

Today, RAF Kumalo is a Zimbabwean Army barracks, with many of the old air force buildings at the entrance of the camp still in use. The runway has been largely reclaimed by the bush. The same applies to the rest of the old airfield, much of it being hidden by head-high grass. The RATG is remembered at the Zimbabwe Air Force museum at Gweru (Gwelo until 1982). Here the story of the more than 10,000 pilots who trained in Southern Rhodesia is told in a couple of ageing cabinet displays. A North American Harvard and a Tiger Moth both proudly wear the green and yellow bars of the SRAF either side of RAF-style roundels. Sadly, like much of Zimbabwe the museum currently looks a little unloved. Perhaps understandably, the aircraft used against the black resistance movement seem to receive the least care, with a Hawker Hunter slowly rusting away in a hanger. No doubt if Gordon Edwards had had the chance to visit today, it would be the dilapidated Spitfire that would have drawn his attention, taking him back to his teenage dreams of flying one and the memory of getting close to such a magnificent machine for the first time on a lonely Scottish airfield.

GORDON'S FIANCÉE

During Gordon's visits home he developed a very close friendship with a local girl. In common with many servicemen, it must have been a challenge for him to maintain this bond given his overseas postings. Gordon was a keen letter writer though, and no doubt this helped the relationship blossom.

Gordon proposed to his girlfriend but, like his decision to join up, he kept this from his domineering mother. It can only be imagined how his lover was counting down the days until Gordon's training was over and how she must have hoped that he would be sent back to the United Kingdom when he had finished in Rhodesia. When the news of Gordon's disappearance arrived she would have had to rely on Gordon's sister, Muriel, for information as she was not formally part of the family yet. Certainly Sarah, Gordon's mother, was too wrapped up in her own devastation to offer any support or consolation.

Gordon's fiancée, like Sarah, never fully recovered from her loss. One would like to think that this was some measure of Gordon's personality; he seems to have been popular with, and loved by, all those that knew him. Gordon stayed in her heart and she never married.

THE HURRICANE OF THE LAKE

Almost exactly sixty years after the murder trial, a direct link to Gordon Edwards emerged from a Russian lake.

Hawker Hurricane Z5252 was one of the crated fighters that had accompanied Gordon's convoy to Russia in 1941 before being assembled by the airmen of 151 Wing. It was the aircraft test flown on 25 September by Major General A.A. Kuznetsov, who was the Commanding Officer, Naval Air Forces, Soviet Northern Fleet. Kuznetsov was an experienced pilot, with many thousands of flying hours, and to mark the occasion Z5252 lost its RAF 'targets', gained red stars and the bort number 01, signifying the first British aircraft to be handed over to the Russians. Initially, Kuznetsov kept Z5252 as his personal mount. However, having first been transferred to a staff flight, Z5252 found itself in the front line within six months.

On 2 June 1942, Z5252 was one of seven Hurricanes involved in a dogfight with a dozen Bf 109s. Hit by four cannon rounds, the pilot, Lt Markov, was forced to make a belly landing on a frozen lake near Murmansk. Fortunately, the weather was still very cold, despite being June, and the ice supported the damaged aeroplane, allowing Markov to make good his escape. He was back with his unit before sunset, where he reported that his aircraft was in reasonable condition and should be recovered. However, when the salvage crew arrived at the lake there was no sign of the Hurricane, which had eventually proved too much for the summer ice. It had sunk to the bottom.

There the Hurricane lay in peace for sixty years, until a search was made for it. This took longer than expected due to the fact that nobody was really sure which of the many lakes it was at the bottom of. Eventually, in August 2003, it was discovered 18 metres down on a bed of moss, amazingly with its canvas intact and the serial number still visible. A year later it was brought to the surface.

With a little luck, this Hurricane will be restored and will serve as a memorial to all those who lost their lives and, perhaps, especially to a young man from Wales who helped to assemble it before being murdered on the other side of the world.

INDEX

Adamson, Walter 5–6, 71, 75, 79, 90,
    92–4, 96–7, 100–1, 103, 107, 109,
    112–3, 115, 119, 143, 150–1, 180–3,
    190–2, 204–5, 209, 212, 215, 220
African Auxiliary Pioneer Corps 33–4
Airspeed Envoy 11, 85
Airspeed Oxford 73, 85–7, 89–91, 94,
    96–7, 100, 102, 109–10, 112–3, 132,
    150–1, 175, 184, 192
Arden-Clarke, Charles 31, 33, 52
Argus, HMS 40

Bangwato 7, 22, 33, 47, 49, 51, 66–7, 70,
    118, 159, 194, 196–7, 208–9, 212
Basarwa 7, 19, 47, 49, 107, 119, 121–4,
    166–7, 170, 179, 181, 185, 187,
    191–8, 200–1
Bechuanaland 4, 7, 11, 17, 23, 29–33,
    35–7, 45, 51–2, 60, 62, 71, 87, 110,
    112–4, 122, 190, 193, 195, 198,
    204–5, 209, 212–3, 217, 220
Botswana 4–7, 19–21, 36, 45–7, 52, 62,
    64, 78, 80, 107, 108, 147, 199, 204,
    209, 211, 213–6, 220–1
Bulawayo 6, 11, 23, 31, 64, 71–2, 75,
    78–9, 81–2, 85, 89, 96–7, 100,
    109–11, 113–4, 191
Bushmen 4–5, 7, 17, 45–7, 49, 62, 65,
    67–9, 109, 117, 122, 185, 190, 192,
    194–8, 200, 208, 212–4

Catterick, RAF 53
Curtiss P-40 Kittyhawk 58, 61
Curtiss Jenny 73

de Beer, K. M. 107, 117, 123, 127, 147,
    151, 164, 173, 177, 179–80, 183–6
Deere, Alan 11–2, 26, 85

de Havilland Tiger Moth 4, 6, 74, 78, 82,
    192, 221
Douglas DC-3 Dakota 192
Dornier Do 24 59–60
Durban 34, 54, 71, 73, 75, 204, 205, 218

Edwards, Gordon 4–6, 12, 13–6, 25,
    27–8, 38–44, 53–7, 60–1, 71, 75, 79,
    81–2, 84–5, 88–97, 100–3, 109–10,
    112–3, 115, 150–1, 180–3, 185,
    190–2, 202–5, 212, 215, 220–3
Edwards, Muriel 13, 202–3, 222
Edwards, Sarah 12–5, 103, 202–3, 222
Egypt 34, 53, 54, 56, 61, 71, 75, 192
Ellenberger, Vivien F. 107, 116, 141, 146,
    149, 156, 193
Empire Air Training Scheme 73
Eves, Alfred 90, 92, 101, 190

Forsyth-Thompson, Aubrey 193–8, 201,
    204
Francistown 50–1, 64, 106, 112–5,
    117–8, 120–1, 123, 139–40, 144–6,
    147, 151, 154, 156, 159–64, 166, 168,
    172, 178, 193, 198, 200, 202, 220–1
Fraenkel, Percy 107–8, 111, 116, 122,
    128, 134–36, 139, 142–3, 146, 148,
    151, 155–58, 160–2, 165–6, 170–1,
    180–3, 209

Gaborone 4, 21, 29, 31, 211
George V 29, 205
Gotha Go 242 60
Grace, Eric 110–3
Guinea Fowl, RAF 82

Hawker Hurricane 25–8, 40–4, 53–4, 58,
    61, 223–4

Hitchcock, Robert 4–6, 215
Hillside, RAF 72, 75, 100
Huggard, Walter 107, 196–7

Induna, RAF 78, 84, 87, 89–90, 100

Johannesburg 51, 71, 114, 117–9, 123, 155
Junker Ju-87 59–60

Kasfareet, RAF 54–55
Kelly, Reginald 107–8, 112, 122, 129, 135, 140, 144, 146, 149, 156, 166, 178–80, 183, 193
Khama III 21, 22, 23, 24, 29, 47, 67
Khama, Ruth 208, 211
Khama, Seretse 24, 47, 208–11
Khama, Tshekedi 24, 30, 33, 47, 49–52, 68–9, 87, 156, 166, 183, 190, 194–5, 197–201, 208–9, 211–2
Kico 119, 144, 146–7, 151–4, 159, 173–5
Kuaxaxa 112, 114, 118–9, 124–5, 128, 130, 133, 143–4, 152–3, 155, 157, 160, 171–2
Kuznetsov, A.A. 42–3, 223
Koetobe, Keree 70, 107, 119, 122, 124, 126, 129–32, 136, 138, 141–2, 153, 156, 161–8, 171, 173, 177, 179, 183–4, 186, 198
Kumalo, RAF 85, 87–9, 94, 96–7, 100, 103, 109–10, 112–3, 119–21, 149–50, 184, 221

Langely, Robert 115–8, 120–2, 127, 162, 173, 181, 186, 198, 215
Leatheart, James 10, 11
Llanstephan Castle, SS 40, 44
Lobatsi (Lobatse) 5, 33, 51, 106, 180, 205, 217
London 6, 15, 25, 26, 27, 51, 52, 102, 196, 197, 200, 205, 208–9
London Missionary Society (LMS) 21–23, 47, 52

Mackenzie, William F. 107, 141, 149, 156, 160, 171, 194

Mafeking (Mafikeng) 24, 48, 71, 106, 108, 180, 196, 197, 200, 201
Makgadikgadi Pans 19, 65, 67
Mamorobe 154, 168, 170–1
Maroto, Anchere 107, 123, 126, 130
Mashupateale, Autwa 107, 126, 130, 132, 149, 162, 173
Mashupateale, Tammai 70, 107, 115–6, 118–9, 122, 124–36, 138–42, 144–49, 151–3, 157–77, 183, 186, 193, 195, 198
Matammai 127, 140, 148–9, 158, 166–8, 170–1, 175–6
Maun 31, 51, 70, 114, 121
Mendi, SS 30
Messerschmitt Bf 109 10–11, 26, 42, 56–8, 60, 223
Miles Magister 10–11
Miskin 13–4, 202–3
Moffat, RAF 72, 82
Molatlhwe, Ephraim 216–8
Molele, Twai Twai 4, 62–70, 107, 114–120, 122–36, 138–40, 142–6, 149–57, 160–6, 168, 172–7, 182–3, 186, 193–6, 198, 200, 209, 212–3, 215
Morobe 115, 119, 122, 126, 130, 133, 138–41, 148–9, 151–2, 154, 159, 162, 168–9, 173–4, 179, 182
Moshweu, Seitshiro 107, 117, 194
Murmansk 38, 40–3, 44, 223

Nata 63, 65–6, 68–70, 110, 114–7, 121, 130, 134, 152–3, 157, 166, 193, 196–8, 200–1, 212–3, 215
Nekate 69, 115–6, 127, 130, 148–9, 158, 160, 166, 167, 169–70, 172
Nonga 158, 167, 169–71, 201
North American Harvard 4, 73, 87–8, 192, 221
Northolt, RAF 25–6
Norton, RAF 80

Patsima 158–9, 168–70
Preston-Whyte, Robert 113, 116–9, 123, 133, 142, 149, 153, 155, 161, 162, 171, 186, 198
Pontyclun 12

Ramsbottom-Isherwood, Henry 43–4
Rekisang 69–70, 115–7, 119, 122, 126,
    130, 132–9, 142, 145–7, 152–5,
    158–9, 162, 164, 165, 169–70, 173–6,
    179, 182
Resetora, Chenda 107, 126–7, 129–33,
    138–9, 141–2, 146–9, 174, 176, 181
Rey, Charles 47–52, 208, 211
Rhodes, Cecil 23, 79–80, 213
Rhodesian Air Training Group 5, 72–3,
    80, 88, 94, 100, 190, 219, 221
Roper, Edwin R 107, 154–5, 158–65,
    167–70, 172–79
Royal Air Force 4–5, 10–2, 15–6, 25–6,
    30, 32, 38–9, 41–4, 54, 57–8, 60,
    72–3, 80, 82, 85–6, 91, 93, 95, 101–2,
    109, 111–2, 117–9, 121, 143, 149–50,
    181, 184, 190–1, 197, 219–21, 223
Royal Air Force Units
    6 Squadron 58
    17 Squadron 39
    44 Squadron 221
    74 Squadron 10
    81 Squadron 38–9, 42, 44
    111 Squadron 25–8, 111
    131 Squadron 61
    134 Squadron 38–9, 42–4, 53, 61
    317 Squadron 32
    504 Squadron 39
    543 Squadron 220
    617 Squadron 93
    151 Wing 38–9, 41, 43–4, 223

Serowe 18, 22, 31, 47, 50, 87, 157, 196,
    199, 208
Shoshong 21–22
South Rhodesian Air Force 72, 74, 219,
    221
Supermarine Spitfire 4, 10–1, 25–6, 28,
    32, 35, 53, 57, 61, 219, 221
Tait, Harry 71, 75, 101, 192
Talifang 158, 167, 170–1, 201
Tee Emm 83, 91
Temee 119, 124–5, 128–30, 135–6, 142,
    148, 153–5, 159, 162–4, 172–4, 181
Thornhill, RAF 82
Toi Toi 119, 125–6, 130, 136, 141–2,
    144, 148, 152–5, 159, 162–3, 173–4,
    176, 181
Tyua (Shua) 5, 46, 64–7, 70, 212–3, 215

Vaenga 40–3
Vickers Valiant 220
Victoria Falls 80, 194

Watkins, Chris 4–6
Watkins, Rosalind 14, 202–3
Witwatersrand Native Labour
    Association 70, 114–5, 117, 125, 153,
    197, 199, 201
Whange, Bene 107, 126, 130–1, 148, 172
Whange, Haukwe 107, 126

Ynyshir 12

If you enjoyed this book, you may also be interested in …

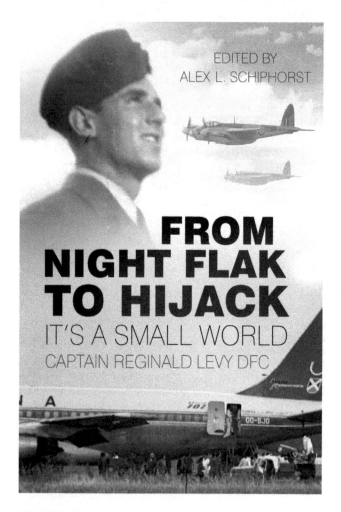

EDITED BY
ALEX L. SCHIPHORST

FROM NIGHT FLAK TO HIJACK
IT'S A SMALL WORLD
CAPTAIN REGINALD LEVY DFC

978 0 7509 6104 2

'. . . there comes out from the sea from time to time a hand of steel which plucks the enemy from their posts with growing efficiency . . .'
WINSTON CHURCHILL

THE LOST BAND OF BROTHERS

TOM KEENE

FOREWORD BY MAJOR GENERAL JULIAN THOMPSON CB, OBE

978 0 7509 6290 2